On Juniper Mountain

A Journey in the Himalayas

First published by O Books, 2010
O Books is an imprint of John Hunt Publishing Ltd., The Bothy, Deershot Lodge, Park Lane, Ropley,
Hants, SO24 0BE, UK
office1@o-books.net
www.o-books.net

Distribution in:

UK and Europe
Orca Book Services
orders@orcabookservices.co.uk
Tel: 01202 665432 Fax: 01202 666219
Int. code (44)

USA and Canada
NBN
custserv@nbnbooks.com
Tel: 1 800 462 6420 Fax: 1 800 338 4550

Australia and New Zealand
Brumby Books
sales@brumbybooks.com.au
Tel: 61 3 9761 5535 Fax: 61 3 9761 7095

Far East (offices in Singapore, Thailand,
Hong Kong, Taiwan)
Pansing Distribution Pte Ltd
kemal@pansing.com
Tel: 65 6319 9939 Fax: 65 6462 5761

South Africa
Stephan Phillips (pty) Ltd
Email: orders@stephanphillips.com
Tel: 27 21 4489839 Telefax: 27 21 4479879

Text copyright Angela Locke 2009

Design: Stuart Davies

ISBN: 978 1 84694 301 0

A CIP catalogue record for this book is available
from the British Library.

Printed in the UK by CPI Antony Rowe

O Books operates a distinctive and ethical publishing philosophy in
all areas of its business, from its global network of authors to
production and worldwide distribution.

On Juniper Mountain

A Journey in the Himalayas

Angela Locke

BOOKS

Winchester, UK
Washington, USA

For Som, who gave me so much understanding, and for
the beautiful people of Nepal

*'Himalaya today remains a sacred place, where our existence recovers
its meaning. A true journey is a mutation. Once marked by it, you
can never be the same as you were before.'*
Maurice Herzog: HIMALAYA

Some names have been changed to protect the privacy of
individuals

I would like to offer a tribute to the pioneering work of Sir Edmund Hillary, that giant among Himalayan climbers, who died in 2008. His Himalayan Trust, founded in 1960 to help Sherpa communities in the Khumbu, is a visionary model of a community-based charity, which has made such difference to the lives of the Sherpa people in Nepal, through their inspiring work which continues to this day.

***

I would like also to extend my special thanks through this book to members of the wonderful Juniper Trust volunteer team;Yvonne Booth, our tireless secretary; Cheryl Frost, our Project Officer; Sarah Thomas, who keeps our finances in strict order; Bikrum Pandey, our long-term Nepal coordinator; Val Pitkethley in Peru, still working with groups of volunteers, between her trekking activities, to put solar panels into villages, and Glenn Rowley, Co-Director of KE Adventure Travel with Tim Greening, all of whom have given us so much support in the last ten years to expand our work. Since KE Adventure Travel has worked alongside us, Juniper Trust has been able to expand enormously through KE's network of connections and trek leaders across the world. They are very generous in giving us the help of staff and facilities. Thanks too, to so many others both here in the UK and in the countries where we are working, who help us in our work, including Geoff Stone and Cotswold Outdoor Clothing who, along with KE, have given us such generous support, to individuals such as Joan Robinson, who have tirelessly raised money for our projects, and schools like the tiny Threlkeld primary school under the shadow of Blencathra, who gave monies collected from the nativity plays in the church at Christmas, and the children of Beaconside Infant School and their Headmistress, my sister Stephanie Fearn, who generously collected for us at their Harvest Festivals, and to countless individuals and groups who have been so generous to us over the years. Of course, also, Ullswater Community College in Penrith, whose Sixth Form expeditions did so much to kick-start links with Nepal, its visionary Headmaster David Robinson, and teachers Maggie, Shaun, and Pete and later Rib, and our first volunteers, Karen Barbier, Amy Holliman and Sara Barnard, who went back the following year after the first Ullswater Expedition to help the work of street children at the ROKPA home in Bhoudinath.

So many thanks also are due for support in those early days of Juniper Trust to Sir Chris Bonington, who kindly agreed to be our Patron, Ailsa Mackenzie, Tony Verity, Dr Andrew Robertson, Neville Howard, Dr Patrick Gray, Michael Josh, Peter Johnston, Ron Kenyon and Bill O'Connor. The moment at an early Juniper Trust meeting when Bill O'Connor, now a leading Alpine and Himalayan guide and author, recognised Michael Josh, who had been his climbing guru in the early 60's in Norway, and embraced him across the table (they had never met again since those early days), was treasured by us all. It sums up the sense of community within Juniper Trust which is so precious. Thank you, too, to Galongma Karma Tsultrim Zangmo for her great kindness to me in enabling me to meet HH The Dalai Lama and Samye Ling monastery in Scotland.

The debt I owe to so many people in Nepal for their inestimable help, kindness and wisdom over the years, is difficult to adequately express. Among so many are Som Bajracharya, his wonderful wife Raati, Bed Prasad Koju, the Mayor of Dhulikhel Mr B.P Shrestha, and Nirmala Shrestha. In the U.K., special thanks to Doug Scott's daughter Martha and her family, who gave me such encouragement to go out to Nepal, and Wendy Bonington, who told me it doesn't matter if I am slow and afraid, but just to do it anyway!

A big thankyou, too, to my wonderful assistant for many years, Diane Scott, who helped me through many dark moments in the writing process of this book, and my current secretary, Sue Catterson, who patiently helped me in the preparation of the final manuscript.

Very special thanks and much love to my husband Colin for all his selfless help and support over the years, including serving time on the current Juniper Trust committee. I couldn't have done any of it without him!

Angela Locke
Cumbria 2009

Preface

For every journey there has to be a first step. When, in 1992, Angela Locke travelled to Nepal for the first time, she had never been anywhere in the Developing World. This first journey would be a life-changing experience which would culminate in the founding of the charity Juniper Trust, of which I am the Patron, which now works to provide basic facilities for the poorest and most disadvantaged communities accross the world. This is a book about an inner journey, not an adventure in a conventional sense, but a journey of discovery nonetheless. No mountains were summitted, but there is real adventure, told against a background of the sublime beauty of the Himalayas and of the gentle people who inhabit the foothills of Nepal.

Chris Bonington
Cumbria 2009

On a beautiful summer's evening, Juniper Trust are gathered for a meeting on the terrace of a house overlooking Keswick in Cumbria. There is much laughter and camaraderie. We sit looking out at the magnificent skyline over the Lake District's Northern Fells – Cat Bells, Grizedale Pike, Causey Pike, Hellvellyn over to the left in the distance, the Jaws of Borrowdale beyond the lake, all lit by the evening sun. A lone hang-glider dangles in the clear sunset sky, floating from somewhere beyond Walla Crag and the craggy outlines of the fells, before disappearing beyond the trees.

We at Juniper Trust are all volunteers and have tiny administrative costs; a model of a small-scale sustainable charity. At this meeting, for example, we agree to support a proposal for solar lights in the Jancopampa and Pamabamba districts of Peru. One hundred and fifty lights at seventy dollars each, which will transform the ability of the village to continue working after dark, whether it is children doing homework or women's craft projects. It is wonderful to think that Juniper Trust is quietly lighting up little bits of Peru in an eco-friendly way. We are also considering support for two doctors, founders of TibetVision, who are setting up eye camps in remote areas of Tibet, removing cataracts and bringing light back into the lives of nomads whose lives were effectively over through the blindness brought on by the levels of ultra-violet light at high altitude. TibetVision is just the sort of small-scale, sustainable community project we can try to help. Tonight we have also been looking at our support for a hostel for children in Ladakh who live too far from school to make the journey daily or even weekly. There are reports too on Balodaya and Ardesha schools in Nepal, and Chobar School for Helpless Children, near the Monkey Temple in Kathmandu, all built with the help of Juniper Trust. There is the wish list from Chobar School to be considered – carpets for baby day care, a reservoir for clean water, a swing, slide and seesaw, balls and skipping ropes, more school uniforms and books. One of our policies, which we have kept faith with since the beginning, is to sustain our support and help, not to walk away, but to continue with our partnerships as long as they are needed. ABVK, for example, a wonderful centre in Banepa, Nepal, for children and adults with severe handicaps, is a new project to attract support from Juniper Trust, after it was recommended by Aidan and Caroline Warlow. Aidan is the Founder-Principal of Kathmandu University High School, and I travelled to Nepal with him and Ailsa Mackenzie in the early days of the founding of Juniper Trust.

Since the beginning, working in a low-impact way, alongside local communities, really listening to their needs, our help can 'trickle up' rather than 'trickle down' to enable change in an appropriate way. We have learned so many lessons from our Nepalese friends, for Juniper Trust had its roots in Nepal, founded after my first visit there. From its small beginnings, it has grown into a worldwide charity.

I think back to that day, nearly eighteen years ago, when I walked into the Post Office in Hesket Newmarket and saw a page open in a magazine advertising a Beginners' Trek to the Himalayas. Did it all begin there or long before? One thing is certain. My life was about to change forever and nothing would ever be the same again...

1

'You in the Himalayas! You must be joking. You can't even find your way round the car park.'

Leaving behind my husband and two teenage children, my fellside farmhouse in Cumbria, friends and neighbours, I am going to Nepal. It will be the first time I have been away by myself, and only the second time I have ever flown. I can't imagine what I was doing when I booked the flight. I am terrified, but I'm stuck with it. Everyone knows, and I have to go, whatever I feel like inside.

Now I am standing at the frozen food counter in Safeways, trying to calculate the number of pizzas my family might get through in my absence. The youngest two are thirteen and fifteen, and at last I feel I can fulfil this ridiculous ambition to go to the Himalayas, crossing my fingers that they can cope. And after all, there is my capable husband to look after things while I am away...

I load up my trolley and trailing rebellious teenagers, who would rather be anywhere but here, I turn to go to the checkout. Standing behind me, in a black tracksuit, is a tall man. Despite the lack of robes, I know I am looking at a Tibetan, though this is Safeways in Penrith, not Dharamsala. I stare at him and he meets my eyes, smiling.

'Excuse me,' I ask nervously. 'Are you a Tibetan?'

I feel a total fool, not helped by the groans of embarrassment from my two teenagers. He looks up and gives me one of those slow peaceful smiles I will come to know so well in my other life; that unimaginable life I am about to embark on.

'Yes, I am Tibetan. How did you know?'

I find myself pouring out the story of why I am going to the Himalayas, my fascination with Tibetan Buddhism, the books I have read, the book I am writing, my admiration for the Dalai

Lama, and this strange, overwhelming compunction I have to see those great mountains. The kids are mad with me.

'Mum, why do you always have to talk to people when you go in a supermarket? You are so embarrassing!'

Nothing stems this terrible outpouring of feeling. The frozen stuff is defrosting, but the Tibetan is still listening. When I finally pause for breath, he tells me he is a monk, teaching English at Conishead Priory in South Cumbria. He invites me to visit one day. I thank him, feeling exposed and foolish, and move away to complete my shopping.

While we are waiting at the checkout, I feel a gentle tap on my shoulder. My new Tibetan friend is standing beside me in the queue.

'I need to tell you something,' he said quietly. 'You must know that the book is not important.'

'*Of course it is.*' I say to myself silently, rebelliously. '*Why else would I be going all that way?*'

He smiles that wise smile once again.

'No, you are wrong. The book is not important.' He pauses. 'But the journey is important.'

And so it begins.

2

In the soulless, marble-floored airport at dawn, a woman guard in a yashmak transfixes me with a machine gun and leads me away. I am totally alone, in an alien world. There is neither time nor opportunity to protest. Weak and dizzy after a sleepless night, I am taken to a room without furniture, and the door is firmly shut. Somehow, inadvertently, on my way to rejoin the plane, I have set off the alarms as I walked through the security check. No one else in the world knows I am here. The rest of the group are scattered, and no one has seen me being taken away.

The woman begins a body search. I hardly dare to move. What if someone has planted something on me? I have heard about such things: a woman travelling alone, naïve, vulnerable. What are they looking for?

'I have nothing! I have nothing!'

Overcome by waves of homesickness, I just want to be home, and safe, with the people I love most in the world. I don't want to be here. It was utterly foolish and foolhardy to come.

She runs her hands over my body. The half of her face that I can see is quite expressionless, the gun inches from my face. I try to stay calm, smile, not to seem afraid.

There are long seconds. At last she points down to my boots.

'Metal!' she says abruptly in English. She indicates that I take them off. She opens the door. Somehow I understand that these kinds of boots, the kind with a metal shank in the heel, can set off the alarms.

I am shaking with relief. Am I really free to go?

The plane is still on the tarmac. Out there, somewhere, those shining mountains still wait for me.

***

We are falling slowly down into a wide bowl of hills, green higher up but browner towards the bottom, terraced and ridged like some mathematical diagram. Every so often there are little pinkish houses with thatched roofs clinging to the hills.

We are actually *here*, at last, after all these months and years of dreaming, but it means nothing to me. Still shaken by my experience at the airport, I can only feel that it is utterly alien. I will never love it.

Below us is a pinkish yellow haze between the mountains, pinkish houses and yellow fields of what looks like rape, and a huge chimney belching pinkish brown smoke with piles of toy bricks beside it; toy houses again in long lines and the silvery snake of a river crawling across the plain. We are coming into the airfield smoothly, the Royal Nepal pilot doing his job well, despite all the jokes before I left about landing on a pocket handkerchief.

There has been cloud most of the way in, and even now we are to be denied a first view of the Himalayas, except for faint shadows of what could have been more cloud. But then, just as we touch down, a window appears in the haze. Quite clearly, one high, white, perfect peak hangs in the sky. I catch my breath with the beginning of something. Then it is gone.

After that, it all goes downhill. I am hot in my tracksuit, weighed down with cameras, hand luggage and a fleece jacket, clumping along in those walking boots which so nearly caused a disaster at the airport.

My handbag keeps slipping off my shoulder, the camera bumping my hip. Anyone catching sight of me will know instantly how much a fish out of water I am. Almost everyone else in the group is a couple, except Adrian, one of our group leaders, whose sticky-out ears and baseball cap are bobbing ahead of me, six inches above everyone else. He lopes along the concrete corridor, a tiny rucksack sitting easily on his back, cool and assured.

Nothing prepares us for the next bit; the melee of the arrival area. My bags, a huge rucksack and big case, both bulging at the seams, are bound to be the last. We all stand here, for what seems like hours in the stifling heat, watching the same three unclaimed bags going round and round. Perhaps they will go round like that forever, until someone takes pity on them.

Then our planeload of stuff begins to appear. Mine isn't there. Hot and faint, I feel tears of self-pity well in my throat. What am I doing here?

A man turns and smiles.

'Hi! I'm Glen. Tell me what your bags look like. You just wait here and I'll fetch them .'

I feel like a little old lady being taken across a zebra crossing.

'Cheer up,' he grins at me. 'This is the beginning of a great adventure.'

My bags arrive at last. I lift them on the trolley Glen has found for me, but it is instantly snatched by one of the ragged porters who prey round us. I am manifestly on my own, despite the moral support. Easy pickings. The porter runs with my trolley to the far end of the hall.

'OK. OK. I take.'

We have been warned about this, but what can I do? And I can't tip him. I have no rupees. He dumps my bag in front of a fearsome customs official, while I trundle breathlessly behind. Bored, the official chalks a squiggle on them both and I am through. The porter pushes my trolley out of the door of the airport. Suddenly we are in blazing sun.

'I get taxi. I help.'

'No! No! I am with a group. Cannot go! Must wait. No rupees. I have no rupees!'

He drops my bags unceremoniously and, with a philosophical grin, he sprints off to find a better deal. At least I am through the doors. The sun clamps down on us. There is an overpowering smell of human bodies, even out here, in the fresh air. A gaggle of children hang about us, filthy faces encrusted with sores, their heads bound with dirty, blood-stained bandages. What can have happened to them? Some awful accident?

'One rupee! One rupee!'

Five ragged boys come up and try to take my trolley.

'*No!* I have no rupees.'

Out of nowhere a man in a tweed jacket appears.

'*Namaste!*' He joins his hands together in a graceful gesture I am too harassed to appreciate. 'Please, you will come this way!'

Another porter come to steal my baggage? I hesitate. He takes hold of my trolley firmly and steers it off the pavement into the road.

'Please. No!'

He takes no notice: only smiles.

There is a coach a few yards away. A woman, cool and blonde in a denim skirt, is waiting there. The others begin to trickle up, half-recognised from the airport in England. They all look as shell-shocked as I feel. The sight gives me perverse comfort. The man in the tweed jacket smiles again. (I have yet to learn that a tweed jacket is the ultimate fashion statement in Nepal.)

'Please!'

It's OK. We are in the right place, thank God. We stand, mutely grateful, stunned by sun, noise and fumes. The begging children come round again, bringing that suffocating smell.

'One rupee! One rupee!'

Will we ever become hardened to this? We stand while Annabel, the cool blonde English courier, consults her list. We are wilted by the hot sun and the long flight and the utter alienness of it all, by the noise and the disorder, the faces of the beggars and the filth. How can we bear it?

Ram (the man in the tweed jacket), directs us across the road to the coach. I stagger on board with my hand luggage, banging my head on the coach roof as I get in, tangled in straps and bags.

For the second time in half an hour I feel the tears come. A dull pain starts in my head. Where are my other bags? I am suddenly too tired to care.

There is an air of shock and depression on the bus. Most of us, I would guess, have never been into the 'Third World'. Maybe this is why we chose this safe little group. The coach starts off with a shudder, scattering begging children, bicycles and taxis. It roars around the roundabout. A cow walks in front of it just as we speed away. I shut my eyes. The coach screeches to a halt. I open my eyes. The cow is sauntering unhurriedly in front of us, two feet from the wheels. It makes its way over to the central island. Bicycles, taxis, mini buses, coaches and two odd-looking, three-wheeled vehicles I can't identify, all come to a respectful stop.

'Can't imagine that happening in Trafalgar Square!' says someone at the back.

3

What is happening to me, in this place? I have a poky room in an indifferent hotel on the outskirts of Kathmandu. There is the incessant noise of horns and a rumble of traffic. The shower head has fallen off and I wrestle with the internal telephone to get it fixed. My lamp flashes on and off at odd intervals. I am irritated and depressed after a day and night without sleep.

Yet something *is* happening to me. I struggle with the grimy window, the mesh outside, which looks like my mother's old meat safe and about as clean. Leaning out into the orange-pink dusk, the sounds of traffic are even louder now. Why does everyone here blow their horns all the time? There is a courtyard, an alleyway, and a row of little shops between us and the road. Evening staff are arriving and leaving in a variety of run-down cars or motor scooters, shouting across to one another. Beyond the courtyard to one side is an office block with lights on in some rooms, and a man looking out. Beyond that I glimpse another four or five storey building with *Microsoft* written on one side, and a giant satellite dish. Next door to that is a temple, gleaming pink-gold in the dying sun. Over the screeching roar of traffic, I can hear the temple bell. Beyond that, and beyond the forest of wires and aerials, is the dim outline of the foothills.

I lean out further, taking in a hesitant breath. The smell of Nepal comes up to me, a totally alien scent. Somewhere in there must be drains, but also aromatic smoke, herbs, some spice. I remember once someone talking to me of 'the scent of India', a dear old friend, a priest. He told me he cried when he arrived in Delhi and begged to be taken back to the airport. Then, six months later, he cried all the way home. Is this the scent of the East, that will capture me and never let me go? It seems a ridiculous thought...

I remember the flowers in front of the statue of Shiva, with those graceful many arms, downstairs in the modern, marble-floored lobby of the hotel; the first thing we saw when we arrived into the coolness. That sharp smell of marigolds. Right there, by the door, a little shrine. I breathe again, half-afraid. That scent; like old churches, but not musty, not dead. What is it? Incense! Warm, alive and exciting; utterly strange. Stretching my arms onto the windowsill, in all the dust, I am surprised at myself.

The man in the building opposite still watches. The sun slips down behind the brown hills. A huge black bird detaches itself from a tree in the courtyard. It circles above me and then it is gone. It looks as big as an eagle; probably a black kite.

Something stirs in me. I stay there, leaning on my windowsill. I should be unpacking. I should go and have my shower. I should write home immediately. The scents of the warm street comes up. I stay looking out at the dusk.

Will I survive this intact? Will I get Kathmandu Quickstep, Hepatitis, Amoebic Dysentery, lice, cholera? Trying to get out of my door and down to dinner, my door chain jams in its track. I have to make another phone call (that women in 402 again!) There is a brief, embarrassing interlude while the bellboy apologetically squeezes his hand through the crack in the door and manipulates my door chain. Brilliant security! If he can do it, so can any intruder in the night. Eventually, he frees the chain.

'Madam! This is always happening. Very sorry. Do not use!'

Very comforting.

'Thank you. Thank you very much.'

By now I have disgusting looking rupees (the paper money is filthy). R.30 is supposed to be right for a tip. I give it to him and he smiles like the sun coming out. About 20p! Is it too much?

I emerge sheepishly. It is almost suppertime but we have to meet for a briefing downstairs. They are all sitting in the hotel lounge, waiting for me. There are fans on the ceiling, like a scene from *A Passage to India,* deep brown chairs, little glass-topped tables, a tray or two left over from tea, silver tea pots. How very English. Yet this is one part of the world which has never been in anyone's empire unless you count the Gorkha. Couples are sitting together with bottles of beer, looking happy and cool.

Annabel smiles at me. 'Hi! We were waiting for you. Hear you got locked in your room!'

Great start.

Cool Annabel tells us things: Don't have ice in your drinks. Don't clean your teeth in the water. Don't eat salads, unpeeled fruit or raw things. We have read it a hundred times anyway. I know my *Trekking in Nepal* inside out, though it doesn't tell you about your door chain jamming.

We go into dinner. I am alone now, but the feeling is exhilarating. Then, instantaneously, guilt replaces exhilaration. I remember the woman at my neighbour's gate before I left. '*I couldn't even go to market without leaving my husband's lunch covered over on the side.*' More fool you for beginning what you now resent, I thought, but didn't say. But I remember her accusing stare. I must ring home later, check that they are OK. In the meantime, there is the minefield of the food to get through without disaster...

We are sitting in a long bare room with one naked bulb, silent again. The waitresses, all Tibetans, stand and watch, hands folded under their striped aprons. Tense with suspicion, we watch as the food is set down before us. A year or more of propaganda – 'Be careful what you eat, keep away from the meat, don't drink the water. Whatever you do watch the cutlery: it's the quickest way to get Hep.' I stare down at the bowl of soup. Unidentifiable things float in it. However, it does smell delicious. I take a tentative sip; tastes fairly good too. Some of the braver souls are eating already. Others watch us apprehensively, as though expecting us to drop dead. I begin to enjoy myself, remembering suddenly that I haven't eaten for nearly twenty-four hours.

More food arrives: rice, noodles, chopped spring onion. I have already decided to be vegetarian this trip. It's all part of the kind of Retreat idea that I had in mind from the beginning; going to the mountains, being changed, whatever, which grew out of all that reading and dreaming. Here, sitting at this long table with these other frightened people, feeling so ordinary and afraid, it seems pretentious and ridiculous.

They bring us black Nepalese tea. The waitresses are quiet and courteous, but the silence sits around us. Just now we are so tired, and it is all too much. One by one we leave. Some of us smile our thanks, embarrassed by our timidity with the food. The girls smile back, put their hands together in that graceful gesture – 'Namaste'. It gives me a warm feeling, like leaning out of the window above the courtyard, listening to the street. I stop by one of the girls.

'Are you from Tibet?'

It gives me a thrill. Tibet. After all those dreams. High places. The Chang Tang plain. The scent of yak dung fires. The Potala, white and gold. It lives in my imagination so strongly I feel it is a place I once knew. Before the Chinese. Anyway, a long, long time ago.

She smiles shyly. 'Yes!'

She is only young. Maybe her parents came out with the Dalai Lama.

'Very beautiful country! Dalai Lama!' I say.

Her face lights up. 'Yes! Dalai Lama!'

Awkwardly, I put my hands together and bow my head.

'Namaste.'

'Namaste.'

The others, still at the table, are looking at me. I feel their eyes on my back. Blushing, I scurry out of the restaurant.

I am very, very tired. I climb the stairs, too scared to use the lift in case it sticks between floors! Dear God, what am I doing here, so far from home, when I am too scared to use a bloody lift?

But then I'm glad I haven't, because in the upstairs restaurant, as I walk past, a Nepalese band is playing; five musicians sitting in the corner among the potted palms. There is a pipe, a sitar and a man with the drums, and one strange, plaintive instrument like a tiny violin. I peek in at the door and the drummer smiles at me. I turn away hastily, and climb three more flights of marble stairs. The music, strange and exciting, follows me, getting softer. I can still hear it when I get to my room, fumble with my key, let myself into the musty darkness.

I feel so weird I can hardly stand. Terribly tired.

'Remember not to clean your teeth in the water!' someone says outside in the corridor. 'See you in the morning!'

I can still hear the sound of the Nepalese band, sometimes closer to me, sometimes further away. Always it intrudes in upon me. Then that lamp will keep switching on and off in a ghostly way. Now I can't use my security chain, I put my rucksack and my big case against the door. But then I worry that if there is a fire and I have to get out quickly, I won't be able to. How foolish these fears will seem in the light of day.

Finally, in desperation, I sit up, fumble with that lethal lamp and squint at my watch. It is eleven o'clock. Nepal is five hours and forty minutes ahead at this time of year (early Spring) and I suppose it is about five-thirty in the evening in England. They should be at home. My husband will be getting supper or lighting the fire, or walking the dogs. The children will be watching TV. Are they alright? How can they possibly be? Trying to remember the codes the receptionist told me earlier, I ring through into the night. After some beeps, I hear the phone ring in England. I imagine it ringing in the dining room. It should also ring upstairs. Either way they should hear it. I wait apprehensively, let it ring twenty-five times, then replace the receiver and try again. There is no reply. I wish I had never thought to phone. Now I am worried. I had made my husband promise to ring me (I had left numbers for wherever we would be) if there was *any* emergency.

Even if I have to fly home. Would he have remembered to pick the children up on time? And if it were snowing (it had snowed before I left – hard to imagine after a day of heat here) would he send them to school anyway, because he wanted to get into the office? (He's pretty dedicated.) And if he hadn't remembered to pick them up, would they have to walk the mile and a half home along that dangerous road, in a blizzard? All this goes round in my head. It's my fault, round and round, and I am too overtired to sleep again.

It is cold now after the heat of the day. I ferret about for my down sleeping bag which everyone told me I wouldn't need. I am grateful for it now, because there is only one blanket and some grey sheets on the bed. Once I am snuggled into that, I do at last go to sleep, lulled by the strange wandering note of the pipes and that twanging haunting violin, the sound of which seems to float around me. Then it bears me away, to some strange mysterious, hardly dreamed about place, and I don't have to worry any more.

4

Standing in line at breakfast with a Buddhist monk in saffron robes no longer seems strange. He lets me go first to the porridge. I eat well: potato cake, scrambled eggs, new baked bread with ham and porridge, and vast quantities of black tea which I am growing to like.

Cool Annabel waits for us in the lobby. I am last as usual. She is talking to a small, dark man who smiles a lot. They seem to know each other well. She introduces us. This is Sharma. He will take care of the group – a kind of cultural guide.

There is a bus waiting for us outside. Sharma leads the way. We are seriously clad in our proper skirts (ladies, so as not to offend the Nepalese) and white safari hats and some of us have walking sticks, and we all have little daysacks with bottled water.

We get onto the bus. Sharma is sitting in the front seat. He has wonderful teeth and a quiet slow smile which lights up his whole face, as though he is bubbling inside with some peaceful laughter. It is probably at me.

I get into a tangle with my camera and my overloaded rucksack, my walking stick and the strap of my hat. I sit by myself. I need the space for all my clutter. I take out the photo-graph of the children and my husband standing by the lake at Rydal Water from the side pocket of my rucksack. It was a happy day out, and even the dog is smiling. I miss them all.

We are going to visit Swayambhunath, the 'Monkey Temple', and then walk back through Kathmandu. I don't like walking in cities or towns. It is very hot. The coach barges along the road and bicycles, taxis and cars get out of the way. We squeeze through the tiny cobbled streets, almost crushing hordes of dark smiling faces in our path. It is chaos. Here too there are little open-fronted shops we have seen before, dogs, cows and goats in the street, and ragged children stopping to stare with their fingers in their mouths or up their noses. Every few yards we come face to face with another bus. There is hardly room for one vehicle, let alone two, so someone has to back up. But everyone smiles.

We climb out of Kathmandu and along a back road. There is some kind of military outpost, with painted red and white poles. Although we have been warned not to photograph military installations, Sharma says it is OK to take photographs here, across the open space which looks like a parade ground. The coach stops so that we can unload and point our cameras, not at the soldiers marching about in the middle of the grass, but because in the distance gleaming on a hill is Swayambhunath, the Monkey Temple. Legend has it that at the beginning of time, Kathmandhu Valley was a beautiful turquoise lake, on which floated a lotus flower, from which shone a blue light, a manifestation of Swayambhu or Adi-Buddha, the first incarnation of the Buddha. Devotees came from far and wide to worship and meditate on the shores of the lake. One such was the sage Manjusri who, wishing to approach more closely, sliced open the valley wall with his Sword of Wisdom. The waters of the lake drained away and the lotus settled on the valley floor. On this spot, Manjusri built a shrine, the sacred site of Swayambhunath.

As we begin to take photographs, a tough-looking soldier in a sort of Ghurkha uniform, comes up to the perimeter fence and taps his swagger stick irritably. He doesn't say anything, but we climb hastily back on the bus. Sharma grins and shrugs his shoulders.

Straight away, I don't like the Monkey Temple, despite the legend. We are besieged by begging children, some with even tinier children on their backs or in their arms. All the babies have bare brown bottoms.

'One rupee! One rupee!'

There are monks in dark blood-red robes, not quite so maroon as those of the Tibetan monks in the hotel. There are also several stalls laid just at the point where I stand, gasping for breath, at the top of the endless stone steps. The stall holders are in Western dress, their tables laden with touristy things – kukri (the Ghurkha knives with carved handles and a serrated edge, horrible when you stab someone with it, I imagine, and worse when you take it out). There are prayer wheels in silver and copper, pipes and odd-looking musical instruments, all laid out on a cloth the same colour as the monks' robes. Sharma is standing by. I explain that I want to buy a silver prayer wheel. He looks at me and smiles.

'If you wish to buy one, please don't ask me if it is genuine silver. At least not in front of the stallholder. I will be too embarrassed to say it is not.'

Then he laughs joyfully, as though it is the best joke in the universe. I find myself laughing too. The prayer flags whip in the wind above us. It is very important to me that I buy a proper prayer wheel someone used and loved (though I don't know if it is fair to buy someone's beloved object. I haven't thought about that yet).

I don't mind this place so much after all, even if it is infested with people like us, but then I see, lying on the steps, a very thin woman with a tiny baby at her breast. We have been told we must not give to beggars, as it only makes the problem worse. The woman and I look at one another as she lies on the step under the handrail. She looks up at me with brown sad eyes and I feel very bad.

There are Hindu statues everywhere, some splashed with red powder or blood. I don't like to think which. I have read and studied quite a lot about Buddhism and I even have a Buddha beside my bed, which the children like and used to bring flowers to, but I don't know anything about Hinduism. We walk clockwise round everything. Sharma explains that this site is very old and that the temple has been here for hundreds of years and all the things tourists want to know, but I can't stop looking at the monkeys with their pink bottoms and their bad-tempered smiles, showing their yellow teeth.

We go inside and mercifully the begging children don't follow, but there is another kind of beggar. The priest is greasy, in a dirty robe. He doesn't give off at all the same kind of feeling that the monks did at breakfast, the one next to me in his saffron and the others laughing at his table in their maroon Tibetan robes. There is a hot smell of fat in this place. The priest demands rupees for having his picture taken after he had already said it was OK. We have to put our rupees into a big box labelled 'Offering Box' in English. I suppose it isn't any different from Carlisle Cathedral Restoration Fund. We shuffle clockwise round in a narrow corridor which is what you are supposed to do. There are sort of statues there, in the gloom, which look very old. It is dark and smoky and I am glad to get out into the sunshine. I thought I would feel special holy feelings, but I don't.

I stand looking over Kathmandu. It is hard to see down into the valley because of the pollution haze. And I can't see the mountains at all. Sharma is standing near, quietly, looking up at the Buddhist stupa. It has gold steps at the top and a white bulb-like dome underneath, and lots of prayer flags. Sharma says that once the Buddha (who was born in Nepal, in the Terai) came here to deliver a sermon. I wonder if he would be sad to see it now, but perhaps he would be more philosophical.

There are flowers strewn on the ground around the Hindu temple, which is alongside, and Sharma tells us about *puja*, a kind of ceremonial offering. If you are a Hindu you do it every morning. Then you get a red spot – a tikka – put on your forehead. There are lots of marigolds and other flowers underfoot, all trampled in the dust and dirt and spit and bits of squashed fruit. I suppose they have been left from making *puja* that morning, before the tourists came.

There are little shrines dotted about the area around the temple. Some are just like flagstones, almost flat with the ground. It would be very easy just to walk over them, which we have been told would be very offensive to the Nepalese people. You must walk round these little holy stones clockwise, so after a bit it gets rather confusing; swirling about in the courtyard like eddies in a stream. But then everyone else is flowing that way too. Perhaps that's what one means by 'go with the flow'. Indeed it would be hard here to walk anti-clockwise. I am worried about accidentally walking on one of these low stones and upsetting the pilgrims. It is just the thing I would do because I wasn't concentrating, and I would feel I had defiled their holy place somehow. I suppose tourists come and walk all over their holy things all the time but it seems awful, like they were sitting casually on a high altar in St Paul's, swinging their legs and eating ice cream.

There are other shrines with statues inside them behind a sort of cage. Rice offerings and rupees have been poked through the bars. I bet we don't give as much out of our incomes to churches as these people do out of their almost nothing to their holy places.

As we turn away from one of the shrines, we catch sight of two small boys climbing furtively down the stonework, reaching their hands inside to grab the coins. And as I look over into the railed-off bit in front of one of the little shrines, I am astonished to see that there are lines of rats marching down the side, making off with the rice offerings. It's a bit like the small boys all over again. Perhaps the Buddha would have laughed at that too.

The Buddhist stupa doesn't seem very atmospheric to me, except for the prayer flags, which are lovely. You can see even from down below that each one has writing on it, a mantra, *Om Mani Padme Hum*. It means 'Hail to the Jewel in the Heart of the Lotus.' The stupas are usually solid. Most of them have holy ashes of some high lama inside. But you can't go in. We just have to remember to go round clockwise.

We climb down hundreds and hundreds of steps in the heat, my hands slipping on the scalding metal handrail. There is a lot of noise and the monkeys swing threateningly above us. There is a golden gate at the bottom like the one at Samye Ling Temple in Scotland – that amazing Tibetan temple by the river Esk. Above the Scottish temple, there are the same golden statues of the Hind and the Wheel.

Then, suddenly we are walking in the real Kathmandu, this rumbustuous, frightening, alive place with all its shocks. There is no bus to protect us. We walk and walk, tired and dusty, trying not to breathe in too much. I wrap my 'yashmak' over my mouth, but still the dust gets through.

We walk back for two hours through the terrible slums. Ashes of dead people on the ghats (riverside steps), pigs rootling among the not-always-perfectly-cremated remains, piles of stinking rubbish, a dead puppy gathering flies, the stench of a suppurating ditch, meat being sold next to the drains and the traffic, children screaming while having their hair washed in water so filthy it hardly seems worthwhile, lepers with stumped arms and no noses begging in the street. Worst of all are the beggars.

Everywhere there are the smells of spices, filthy sewerage, human dirt, car fumes, dust. I hate the stinking river, nearly empty now before the spring rains and full of dead things, and I hate the funeral pyres, the dogs, the terrible traffic fumes, the poverty.

'Buy bangles, really cheap!' The cold touch of a child's hand on my arm, brown eyes, runny nose. Sharma walks far ahead of us and we only keep together because we can spot each other's shining white hats a mile off, like some last little outpost of Empire. Once I catch up with him and ask him about the buildings around us. Even the most crumbling building has carvings. He takes my questions very seriously.

'The buildings are very, very old. This is the really ancient part of the city.'

I want to say to him, I hate all this, this squalor, this poverty. How can you live with it? But it would be very rude.

'The vegetables are so green!' I say at last.

And they are. On the street stalls the spring onions glow like jewels. Unfortunately next to them is a carcass of some animal, raw side out, just being cut up on the pavement, and a pile of hooves and horns underneath a table. I am glad I have decided to become vegetarian. Sharma sees me looking in horror. He smiles his slow smile.

'Many visitors become vegetarian,' he says in his soft, lifting voice.

We have stopped in the sharp sun. The light is behind his head and I can't see him clearly, even when I squint. I wonder how he knows what I am thinking.

My reading comes in useful at lunchtime, when we have an hour to find our place for lunch. As we had come past I had seen a sign for The Yak and Yeti, which I had read about in *Tiger for Breakfast*. The hotel was founded by a Russian called Boris. The others aren't too keen, but I lead them all across the lethal traffic and down an alleyway with shops and suddenly there it is, looking so civilized.

I get the credit for finding it. It is an amazing place; marble floors and dark wood carvings and the Nepalese men in reception wearing startling white shirts. An old Ghurkha in full uniform salutes you at the door. I know I shouldn't feel comfortable about this.

The lobby is a glamorous place, with mini-buses arriving and gear being unloaded with expedition stickers all over it. Sun-bronzed men and women stride in with that far-away, blue-eyed look which explorers and sailors always seem to have (not that I know too many explorers). Men and women advance upon each other across the marble floor, shaking hands firmly, looking into each others' eyes and saying 'Good to see you!' with slight foreign inflections and 'We last met in Brazil. '82, wasn't it?' You can't believe this is really happening in the last decade of the twentieth century. Apart from the trainers and the gruesome jeans and the T-shirts with International Everest Expedition 1992 or some such blazoned across them, this could be out of Kipling. I am impressed, but Adrian, who is the group cynic, says they probably got their T-shirts in the Kathmandu bazaar and it's all a big pose.

I like the juxtaposition of the fax machine going constantly in the lobby, the old fashioned bellboy who takes care of my bag when I ask him, the ancient-looking carvings and all this high-tech equipment, a sense of exploring and new territories. How do these glamorous people manage to look travel-stained and smooth at the same time, when I am just conscious of being travel-stained, with no glory?

We are all in a state of shock with what we have seen, and dehydrated. I order tea and beer and bottled water and drink it all. It is $110 US a night here for a single room. I am not too good on dollar conversions but that sounds a lot. But we decide we will come and have dinner here right at the end.

When we get back to the hotel, I leave my trainers outside the door. They have seen too much. I stand under the shower for fifteen minutes, but I feel I will never be clean. Because it is Sunday in England, I manage to get through to my family on the telephone and speak to them all. Oh, the blessed relief to hear them sounding so normal. But I forgot to ask about the dog (she's pregnant). Then I go down into the lobby and order a beer and write a long, long letter home.

5

Pashupatinath. The name breathes a sigh.

Already we begin to think the word *holy*. How can that be in all this; the dirt, the squalor, the street life, the dead dogs? But it is here, all around us; the monk at breakfast helping himself to scrambled egg, the flowers newly made every morning in the lobby beneath the many-armed Shiva, the joining of hands, the dead dog in the street as much as the flower. I begin to think in ways which stir me, and frighten me.

We walk the cobbles down to Pashupatinath. This little group in our white hats. Not like pilgrims. The women sit on the ground, the old women with the babies, looking up at us. A beggar whines, stumps for hands. We move away. There are marigolds everywhere, dung, thin dogs, a constant noise of chatter. And somewhere, someone is singing, a high, thin song. Sharma calls us and we fly to him, white-hatted, huddled into our group, our backs to the beggars. He tells us this is a holy place, holy like Swayambhunath, but only for Hindus, where they come to make the most sacred *puja* of all. This river (which we cannot yet see) is a tributary of Mother Ganga, and here Hindus come to purify themselves. And to die.

To die here is to be in a state of grace. So if you know you are going to die – if you feel it, with some deep, instinctively wisdom most of us have forgotten – you don't hang on screaming on the edge of the pit, knuckles white. When you are ready to leave, with grace, you come here. Loving friends carry you, or family, and you wait until it is your time.

There is a great golden bull in front of this holy place. The steed of the Lord Shiva, we are told. And we must go no further. We are not Hindus, none of us, and can never be. I didn't know till now that you can only be born a Hindu, but not made into one. So none of us can ever go in.

We stand and stare.

Then we walk over the bridge, which is also holy but not as holy as the temple, because people like us can walk over it without committing sacrilege. Sharma tells us that this is the only place in Nepal where marijuana can be smoked legally, so the holy men (the sadhus) traditionally came here to smoke it. Then, in the seventies, other travellers came too, for their own ends. Not for holiness, but to find their own little visions of the world.

We climb stone steps in the sun. Coming out of the noise, and my confusion (because I don't understand), I feel a strange sense of peace. I like the old grey stone and the trees, the dirty, holy Bagmati River which snakes beneath the bridge. We stop half-way up some steps and here is a square stone archway high up on the bank. Inside is a little stumpy lingam. Pilgrims have been here before me and there are flowers. I look through. It is as though I am looking into an endless mirror. Beyond this stone archway there is another and another and another, going on and on in a perfect straight line along the bank, above the sacred river. Inside each is a lingam just like the last. It is the most perfect thing I have ever seen, this endless reflection, and someone must have told me, because I know it, and didn't know it before, that this is an image of Creation. Shiva is the divinity of destruction, and also of regeneration, endless perfection perpetuated; a perfect metaphysical poem of the Universe.

I stand quietly as the others go away, looking into this silent, ancient, reflected world, remembering my mother's triple mirror. When I was a child, I would sit in the green darkness and move the parts of the mirror back and forth, until I could see myself dimmer and dimmer and greener and greener, shot through with rainbows and light. Until, finally, I could see myself no more.

When I come into the world again, everyone is far ahead with cool Annabel. I am almost alone. Only Sharma waits quietly at the bottom of the steps to see I am not lost. We walk up through the dappled shade to join the others.

After this, I will never be the same. I don't know yet that I will say this again and again while I am in Nepal. I don't know that this is only a beginning.

We climb up higher until we come onto a terrace with a seat, overlooking the whole of this part of the river. I sit a little way apart from the others, half-listening to Sharma who is talking to the group, looking down at the temple steps on the far side of the river. Monkeys are sunning themselves on the roof of the temple. Some are lying out like sunbathers on a beach, scratching their armpits and screeching and the babies are making a nuisance of themselves. Some of the monkeys are playing a game. Like little Tarzans, they swing down on creepers from the cliff face, which is beyond the temple in a narrow gorge, and the babies copy them. They land on a wooden structure in the middle of the river, with jumps so huge that I keep thinking they will fall in the river, then onto the temple steps. From there, they run up among the pilgrims and onto the temple roof. I love the baby monkeys, yet I am very anxious, watching them, that one of them will fall into the dirty holy river, though I suppose they can swim.

The temple steps are shining like it has been raining, but only because people are constantly washing themselves here for purification, making this special *puja*. They come down, these women in their bright saris and the men in mostly western clothes, squatting by the bottom step and dipping their hands in the water, spreading it on their faces and their arms. Some of them throw red and orange flowers in the slow-moving river, mostly marigolds. In the middle of the steps three people have set up an altar. They seem to be making a wreath, ringing bells and burning incense. I don't like to look too closely because it is a personal thing. I feel rather uncomfortable watching. But they don't seem to mind that it is all in public. Most of this is for sad things, yet it all seems wonderfully happy.

In fact, the flowers and the bright saris, the water shining and the monkeys playing Tarzan on the bank, the temple bells ringing round the narrow valley, is the most joyful thing I have ever seen. I feel it even sitting on this bank high up, not part of it because I could never be a Hindu even if I wanted to, and I could never even begin to understand.

But even from the outside it is wonderful. I look outwards and there are other stone temples and smoke rising from further down the bank from a burning pyre: a huge pile of straw and wood, burning very brightly with a huge flame. People are standing round and the smoke is going up into the sky. There are pigeons and doves flying. The smoke from the burning ghat flies up with the sound of the bells and the doves, up above the high valley, into the bright sky.

6

We settle ourselves down, facing the sacred Bagmati River, high up on the valley side above Pashupatinath, looking down on a scene on the temple steps which cannot have changed for hundreds of years. Here we sit, seriously intent, facing Sharma. His skin glows against a white shirt, sleeves rolled up to the elbows. He looks at us, it seems, for the first time, and for the first time we look at him. He is radiating serenity. Perhaps he is happy here.

Then he begins to tell us a little about the religions of Nepal. He pronounces it differently from us: Naypaal, long musical syllables which sing. I begin to listen. For the first time he talks to us, not about ancient architecture or dates of temples nor all the facts and figures he knows he should tell us, but living things. I could not write it down. But I listen and begin, again, to be changed – to have a little insight. Looking at Sharma, I hear what he says.

Clive is feeding a monkey on the wall. It sits and waits while he lines up peanuts along the stone balustrade. The monkey follows behind, grabbing the nuts and baring its teeth, coming right up to us. I move to the far end of the group, nervous because I know monkeys bite and they may carry rabies. When the peanuts have all gone, the monkey gets very upset and begins to scream, following Clive along the wall and trying to jump on his back. He speaks sternly to it but it won't leave him alone.

Sharma talks on. Looking down at the red and orange saris, the wreaths floating on the sacred river, the baby monkeys jumping, I feel I will always love this place, because here I began my understanding.

It is entirely peaceful. Over the river beside the temple, Sharma tells us, is the hospice where the very sick come when they know they are dying. They wait here so they will be in this holy place at the time of death, and thus they can be cremated here. There are stone columns like in a Roman temple. People are just standing about and chatting, and others are laid out in the sun. I do not know if they are dead or not. But further down on the ghats, the body is still burning on the pyre.

We leave the riverside and begin to climb up yet more steps in the hot sun. I have run out of film and someone lends me a spare roll. It takes time to find a patch of shade and I fall behind again. Catching up, the steps are steep and I puff and pant getting to the top, wishing the others weren't so fast. We pass little temples on the right hand side, with shady trees in the courtyard. It must be wonderful to look down always on that scene of perpetual holiness, to hear the bells, and to watch the doves fly up and land in their endless cycle of movement into the sky.

There is another monkey on the wall, playing with a plastic bag, the sort which, in England, would have a printed notice on it saying that it can cause suffocation and should be kept away from children. This monkey is young, but I don't feel I can remove it. As I pass, it bares its teeth at me and screams. Then it rips the plastic bag with its human fingers and gallops away to the far end of the wall, where it sits on a pillar and watches me pass.

We are walking now on the flat. There are yet more shrines and temples in a courtyard on either side of the path. They all feel very ancient, the kind of buildings you might come upon in a jungle, where you uncover an ancient civilization no human has seen for thousands of years; something out of *Raiders of the Lost Ark*. Old grey stone with its knobbles worn smooth, faded statues with blurred faces. There are huge Boudhi trees, like plane trees, and a dapple of ancient shadow and light – an Impressionist painting of a Paris boulevard. And a great quiet. There are people about, but the stone, ancient and alive, absorbs them all.

On one side, between two of the great stone shrines, two small children are standing, watching us. They smile and shout 'One rupee! One rupee!' and one of them holds up a puppy for us to see. It is very thin and wriggles. The girl laughs and holds it upside down. I'm sure that can't be good for it. They run away between the shrines before we can speak to them, their laughter ringing around the stone.

We walk on down a wooded path till we catch up with the river, winding sluggishly across a flat plain which stretches into the distance to misty hills. It smells quite bad, We have to cross it, but the 'bridge' is a block of concrete suspended over a shallow ditch. Although it is no more than six feet above the river, I am apprehensive of falling in. The smell of the water is overpowering. I remember my Uncle Philip fell into the Sweet Water canal in Egypt during the war. He never quite recovered. Yet if this is the same river – the Bagmati – as at Pashupatinath, pilgrims come huge distances to bathe in its waters for purification.

On the far side is a sandy path. We are outside the city, walking through countryside. It's quite different – thatched huts beside the path, bright green and yellow crops in the fields. Women are working on their plots in front of their houses. I ask one of them if I can take her picture. She is so beautiful in her dark red sari, a big gold stud in one side of her nose and a beautiful smile like Sharma's. Gracefully she says to me 'Namaste!' I feel uncomfortable about taking her picture, as though it makes a distance between us.

We walk on in the hot sun. There are stenches from the stagnant ditches, and dust gets in our mouths. Once or twice we stand aside respectfully while a water buffalo ambles past with its huge, golden-brown horns. Women and men (though mostly women) are carrying loads of grass and leaves in wicker *dokos* on their backs. They have a strap across their foreheads, a *tumpline* just as I have seen in the pictures in my guide book. Each of them, laden down with their huge loads, stands aside gracefully for us to pass. They smile and greet us with joined hands 'Namaste!' Encumbered in my own way, with walking stick, camera, micro-recorder, sunhat, bumbag - containing passport, money, tissues, airline tickets, credit cards, which we have been told we should carry with us at all times, throat sweets and emergency Imodium capsules - I reply 'Namaste!' We are getting less self-conscious about it and it is such a charming, happy, peaceful greeting I wish we could do it always. In England when I greet someone, I never quite know what to say. I have never got the hang of it. 'How are you?' seems to demand a reply somehow, as though you thought they meant it, which they generally don't, and in a queer way you are left hanging in mid-air. So 'Namaste!' will do me very well. I think it means 'Welcome. Peace be with you. Greetings to the God within you', certainly that is what it feels like. I am warmed by it and feel welcomed, and the act of joining hands in the air is like the beginning of yoga. We definitely ought to adopt it in England. However, I can't see it having the same effect in a Safeway's queue, though you never know.

Sharma and cool Annabel are far ahead. I walk with a new friend, Sue. On this path (I shall have to remember that this is a *trail*. Anyway, it sounds more glamorous) we tell each other things from the beginning which in ordinary conversation we would not approach for weeks back home. I find her gentle and perceptive.

We are going to Boudhinath, walking through these fields of mustard, potatoes and spring onions which look so fresh and new in the buttery valley light, but are actually watered by this scummy water which flows alongside us, hitting us with its powerful stench. I wish I had worn my serious walking boots instead of light trainers, especially when we have to cross a stretch of shallow river on the path and the stepping stones are very wobbly.

Boudhinath is where many Tibetan refugees live, and is a place very holy to Tibetan Buddhists. I am excited. If I felt so moved at Pashupatinath with the Hindu temple, how much more will I feel now, among the Tibetans?

Suddenly I am in the town again. There are no suburbs as there might be in England, just the backs of proper houses straight after the fields, with a man relieving himself into the stream quite unselfconsciously, though we are embarrassed. Round the corner of the backs of the houses is a crowded street full of Western-type traffic, buses, jeeps and bicycles, as well as all the other sorts of Nepalese traffic. Four or five water buffaloes are gambolling about in the middle of the road like spring lambs, under the doubtful control of one small boy with a stick, and there are those curious three-wheeled taxis like ancient Reliant Robins, and lots of bicycle rickshaws.

We cross the street, dicing with death, this little line of white-hatted Europeans, a little more blasé now about the dangers after a day in Kathmandu. After all, if the traffic can stop for a sacred cow, it will surely stop for us, though I am not entirely certain about the relative importance.

Then we are through an archway, away from the traffic, and despite the crowds of people, I am once again aware of that sense of peace, though it is bedlam as well. It is a little town in here. Stallholders are selling kukri, bangles, flutes and prayer wheels. The stalls are ranged along the walls.

There is a kind of inner wall, and we follow the crowds, all walking clockwise. I must say Sharma and Annabel don't seem too bothered about getting separated from us, which would be very easy in this crush. Fortunately the white hats stand out pretty well.

A quarter of the way round is a small temple which looks just like Samye Ling, except it isn't in the Scottish hills but here, jammed up into this dense little corner. As we wait in the heat to see if we can go inside, Sharma tells us it is closed for prayers. Three little novice monks in maroon robes are playing cards in the entrance. A huge crowd is jammed up against the inner wall outside the temple – children, men and women, all with Tibetan faces. I squeeze through. There in the middle are three Indians with snakes, playing pipes. A cobra is rearing up, swaying by its basket. I watch fascinated. When I come away and tell the others about it, someone points out how cruel it is to the snakes, which of course it is. I am ashamed not to have thought about that. I had been so entranced by the strange hypnotic music, and the frightening feeling of being so near that bat-winged, venomous, powerful head of the cobra which swayed about looking at the crowd. It must be dreadful for the snakes shut up in those wicker baskets.

We shuffle round in the clockwise crowd until we get to the big steps leading up to the great stupa. It is like Swayambhunath, yet utterly unlike. This whole place is so peaceful. It seems clean and quiet, although there are so many people. It's the final days of the Tibetan New Year festival and hordes of smiling pilgrims in bright clothes are climbing the steps to the great white dome. Bells are ringing everywhere. We climb up too, into the free fresh air. It must be high up here, and after the stuffy smelly plain, clear and cool. Prayer flags snap in the wind like Regatta day at the Yacht Club, and there is the same feeling of expectation. A group of maroon-robed priests are stirring great copper bowls, and I peer inside. There are what look like marigold petals floating in a reddish yellow liquid. But Sharma tells me this is saffron, being made into a dye to be splashed onto the stupa during the festival (Both Marigold and Saffron are used as a dye by the Tibetans). Priests squatting by a low table are making an offering. There are bells and shining pots, and by the steps of the stupa, a white painted elephant looks out towards the distant mountains. I stop and, turning away from the stupa, follow its stone gaze. Far away, beyond the yellow, red, green and white Tibetan houses, the yellow, red, and green blouses, the prayer flags and the priests in maroon robes with their saffron, I glimpse those distant, perfect, white peaks against the blue sky.

In the fresh wind I can almost smell the snow.

I turn back to the stupa, dazzling white in the sharp spring sun, daubed with saffron dye, its prayer flags faded to a glowing transparency like stained glass. Adrian picks up one from the ground and examines it. Over and over, mantras are printed on translucent cloth,so the wind will blow through them and the shout will go up to heaven. Adrian pockets the prayer flag, which seems wrong to me. But who am I to say, when I am hoping to buy a prayer wheel which someone once used and loved?

Sharma, standing behind us as we crane our necks to look up at the stupa, tells us that those golden steps at the top are the thirteen stages to Nirvana. There, beneath, are the huge eyes we have seen regarding us dispassionately from the stupa at Swayambhunath – the eyes of the Buddha or the Eye of the Consciousness, I don't know which.

A group of Tibetan women are sitting against the wall, and as I turn to look at them they start to giggle. I must look strange with my black and purple rucksack and my silly hat. I smile back at them and ask if I may take their picture. Like naughty school children unable to control their mirth, they explode with good-natured laughter, leaning against one another and covering their mouths. I can't help laughing too. They are all dressed up to the nines in red blouses and their best striped aprons; their hair oiled smooth and coiled into plaits and buns. I think how beautiful and graceful and gay they are in their New Year clothes, while I feel so awkward and out of place with my white legs and my white socks and my serious skirt. These women are just entirely natural, full of colour and joy; sitting here like bright flowers against the wall, clutching their plastic carrier bags (Rothman cigarettes), giggling and laughing, because today is a holiday and they are here, at Boudhinath. That is enough.

I still have a burning desire to buy a prayer wheel. Annabel tells me that Boudhinath is the best place, and as Sharma is not doing the walk back, he will come with me and help me choose a good one. Not from the stalls, she says. We say goodbye to the others, not envious of their having to walk back in the dust and heat. We will catch a bus instead.

We go through the crowds to a little shop. Unusually, it has a door and we duck inside. I untangle myself enough to put my hands together to say *'Namaste'*, and Sharma shakes hands with the owner. He is about Sharma's age, dressed in Western clothes, like Sharma, white shirt and casual trousers, small and dark. A tiny shop with things in glass cases. We are given stools to sit on. The shop owner is very attentive. However, I wonder if I am about to be ripped off, and whether I will know.

Sharma turns to me.

'This is a very special shop. It is run by my friend. You can trust him. Here is not like the tourist stalls. Here you will get proper value. And while you are here, I will show you something special.'

I am trapped by their courtesy. Sharma speaks to the owner, who slides a tray out from under the counter. On it, under glass, is a wonderful painting on cloth.

Sitting on white clouds, a myriad little Buddhas are enshrined in endless perfection, detailed flowery heavens under an immaculate blue sky, rainbows and arches. Lotus petals, or flames, lick the hem of the Buddha's robes. It is like a picture I have seen of the great thangka which is hung out once a year from the walls of the Potala Palace in Tibet. That is, before the Chinese came. Maybe they don't allow it now. So many different miniature pictures worked in gold and at the centre, is the Buddha.

Sharma says. 'This is a thangka. A religious painting. Buddhists use this as an aid to meditation.'

I wonder why he has taken time to show me this. But then I don't yet know Sharma very well. It must be priceless with all that gold and the wonderful workmanship. I hope the shop owner is not thinking I am a rich Westerner. I don't know how to say I can't afford to buy it without offending him. But then,

Sharma reads my thoughts:

'This thangka is the very finest; you will not see another so fine in a long time. Very, very old. The painting is on both sides. See. It is very rare, but it is not for sale. I just wished you to see it.'

'It is very beautiful. Thank you.'

I look again into the heart of the thangka; lotus flowers and golden Buddhas, endlessly repeated in a formal circular dance; clouds and flowers spinning round, and a golden wheel, like the Wheel of Law on the temple roof at Samye Ling. Each picture so fine and small and infinite, going on and on for ever, like the Shiva lingam shrines at Pashupatinath. Then I think that cannot be because that is Hindu, and this is Buddhist. Another mystery.

The two men are bending over the glass. Sharma begins to show me the golden pictures, to explain a little for my western mind. There is a feeling of quiet in the little shop. I would almost say *reverence*; these two gentle men, and me in my hat, clutching my bumbag. Yet I feel it, this reverence, this rare beauty, a little of the holiness of a much-loved, sacred object. I am glad it is here, in this little shop and that it is not for sale.

I think then that I should *not* buy a prayer wheel. But the thangka is slid away again under the shelf. The proprietor draws aside a sliding glass door and brings out a very simple wheel, made of some sort of wood and horn, like tortoiseshell. It is worn smooth and when Sharma spins it for me, it is lopsided, squeaking like an old bicycle. Sharma says that is because it is old.

'This has been used many times. A good simple prayer wheel. See. Yak horn. And here, a Tibetan wood – I have forgotten its name.' He leans over to show us. Then he takes off the top and shows me that inside is a tight roll of discoloured paper. He looks at me. 'The prayer wheel on the market stalls will have also paper inside, but the prayer will not really be written. If you wish for a prayer wheel for genuine reasons, you must have one where the prayer is *really* written.'

I like this prayer wheel very much; its old brown patina, the way it squeaks, the worn silver round its base. And Sharma says it is not expensive – R.300.

That is about £4, for something that was loved. He says that this prayer wheel is the best for me. But as I hesitate, I see on the shelf a perfect small prayer wheel, Tibetan silver with coral and turquoise just as I have imagined. Sharma says it is expensive. About R.2,000, but old Tibetan silver. Not too old because such holy objects must not be exported beyond a certain age, but about fifteen years old. It has been well used too, and it squeaks in that strangely restful way. I can feel it is Tibetan. The coral and the turquoise and the fine filigree tell me. Yet I feel too that Sharma would like me to have the simple wheel, the kind that every Buddhist monk will carry, along with his bowl and his thangka for meditation and nothing else in the world. So I try to explain awkwardly.

'I love this little wheel. It speaks to me. If I could, I would like to have both.'

Sharma nods.

'This wheel too has been used. It is not just for the tourists.'

And suddenly they smile and seem to understand. We are friends. Not on opposite sides. I also understand, by some process of osmosis, that this is not a place for bargaining. I spin the wheel on its fragile silver stalk and it turns in my hand, peacefully. I can imagine that I will use it too, in my own way.

Sharma shows me that this prayer wheel, which also has at its heart the endless, circular prayer of Tibetan Buddhism which we have seen carved on the Mani stones – *Om Mani Padme Hum*. One thousand times. As the wheel is turned, so the prayer will go up to heaven, or will be scattered to the winds, as with those prayer wheels we saw being turned at the base of the stupa, worn smooth by endless hands. Now I have seen the golden thangka, I can understand a little more why the prayer wheel spins.

The proprietor wraps my two prayer wheels in rice paper. As we leave the shop, I ask Sharma, rather shy of intruding on his private life, whether he is a Buddhist.

'Yes, I am. My father is a Buddhist priest. And my wife is Hindu. That is not so unusual in Nepal. We are very understanding of each other's religions.'

I want to ask more, but we are in the crowds again. I look up at the great stupa, and think that this great dome, in the centre of this wall, these houses, and these mountains, these pilgrims who endlessly walk round clockwise praying, are like some great thangka painted by a god, while the whole world spins and is yet held still. I do not know where these thoughts are coming from, but once again I seem to be at the beginning of something new, yet very, very old.

7

My hair is sticky with dust, and I stand under the hot shower for ten minutes. In the absence of a hairdryer, I go in search of a sunny balcony where I dry my hair. There are lots of corridors in this hotel, and a confusing number of doors. Eventually, I find a door which leads to a balcony overlooking the back of the hotel. It is a different world up there, looking out over the rooftops towards the foothills. I sit on the ground among the pipes, a mobile airer with a couple of vests hanging out to dry, some old garden furniture and a few rush mats. It's hot and I am happy, drying my hair in the sun.

When it is almost dry, I lean over the balcony and look into the back gardens of the houses where there are bicycles and vegetable plots, and a woman in a sari pulling up spring onions in one of the gardens. She bends gracefully, tenderly laying the long green shoots and shining white bulbs of the onions along her arm.

Below me, bougainvillea drapes a trellis, and there is a square of emerald grass. I look across the low roofs of houses towards the back of a temple, towards the hills. Unexpectedly, cloud dissolves into white mountain in the distance, and I stand entranced, looking at a wall of jagged, gleaming ice, framed by orange bougainvillea and the old red brick of a garden wall. A warm wind blows up from the town with all its scents. I stand looking for a long time, close to tears.

Tomorrow, we are going up into the foothills, on the Tibet road, to the little town of Dhulikhel. I find my way to the Indian supermarket on the street and buy bottled water much cheaper that in the hotel, tins of Coke, tissues, loo paper and all essentials of life to sustain myself on the edge of civilization.

I have also explored the back lobby and read the displays on *Waste Management*. There is a conference going on in the hotel, trying to address Kathmandu's terrible litter problem. The aim is to start an education process and impetus for change from the bottom, not the top. The sweepers (who are not very effective at the moment) could be encouraged to collect and sort valuable rubbish. This would contribute to their income which is very low, and as Untouchables might also improve their status. Children too, could be encouraged to educate their parents.The real change in attitude is what, hopefully, might begin to address the problem, the scale of which has just mushroomed over the last few years. At one time, with only a few people living in Kathmandu Valley, rubbish got dumped in the river and eventually floated away or just decayed. The kind of rubbish would have been different too. There would have been less paper and fewer tins, much more bio-degradable. We tourists must be making it all so much worse with our high-class junk.

I am reminded of the old farmer who used to own our farmhouse, telling me that years ago all the rubbish just got thrown in our beck (stream). There was no problem at all. 'Folk nivver worried about it.' But of course, in just the same way, there were very few families living in our valley then. Mother Nature could absorb a bit of detritus without causing an environmental crisis. Now, suddenly she can't, and for us all, habits have to change.

While Sharma is supervising the loading of the luggage, we sit on the wall, soaking up the sun, laughing about inconsequential things. Someone confesses to wiping the light switch with an antiseptic wipe before turning it on. How fearful we still are!

We climb on the coach. Sharma is there, quiet, efficient. I have brought my prayer wheels with me, wrapped in rice paper. Annabel asks me if I am feeling better. I am beginning to like her. She can't help it if she always looks so good, so in control.

Axle deep in sand, lurching over hardcore, we stop and start on our way up to Dhulikhel. The road deteriorates fast into something which seems little more than a track. Still Indian, and now Chinese, trucks and buses speed heedlessly past us, down into Kathmandu. Is this normal, and if so, how do the passengers, cargoes and back axles stand it day after day? This is the road the Chinese built, part of a tit-for-tat arrangement whereby the Indians build a road up to Kathmandu from the Indian border, the Chinese build one down from the Tibet border; the Indians construct a hydro-electric scheme in the South, the Chinese construct one in the North. I hope the Nepalese people are the winners in the end, and aren't just squeezed out.

We stop around late lunchtime in a lay-by on a tarmac section of the road. We have hardly been travelling for more than a few hours, yet it seems like a day. As always in our journeys so far, it is not only distance we have travelled.

So we're here. There's an empty stretch of road, no trucks for the present. On the opposite side of the road, a hillside thick with vegetation looms above us, some brick steps and a few thatched huts, half-hidden in trees. So quiet. Looking down and down, we see that we are floating high above the lower foothills. Only a few ridges are higher than us. There, again, far distant, is the light of those impossible snows, gleaming on the horizon

I suppose we have climbed a long way from the Kathmandu Valley, which is about 4500 ft. But when I get off the bus with all my hand luggage, I am very dizzy, my heart going mad in my chest. I have to cross the road like an old woman, one step at a time.

On the far side is a brick staircase leading steeply upwards. I don't know how I am ever going to make it. Perhaps it's just the strain of the day, and it is very hot. I can feel the sun hammering down, relentlessly.

I try the steps, but I am utterly defeated by this strange sense of weakness, and forced to sit down three steps from the bottom. Sharma is coming up with some luggage. He stops and gives me his slow smile, asking me if I am OK. I smile back, weak and self-pitying.

Someone brings me a cold Coke, I take a few deep breaths, and a sip or two. Magically the dizziness leaves me, my heart stops racing (must write to Coca Cola) and in a few minutes, I feel really well. It's lovely here – glowing flowers beside pink paths, and everywhere the sound of water. I breathe in the thin, clear mountain air and look out over the foothills shimmering in the sun far below. Forest and pale earth stretch away beneath us, woven into crumpled cloth.

Later we sit on a balcony with a dining room behind. I can see, beyond the terrace, that those straw-thatched huts I glimpsed from the road are scattered everywhere, linked by brick paths. Each one looks over the valley. I amble down the path in the hot sun, looking for my room, between rows of sweet peas. Somewhere a bird calls, like water over stone. I feel light and peaceful, though a little strange after the attack of dizziness. I wonder, however, how I will manage the walk which we are to undertake this afternoon, the first little 'trek' of the trip.

My room is almost at the end of the huts, sparkling clean with big windows looking out over the hills. There is a posy of flowers on the little table. It looks so clean that I take off my dirty trainers and leave them by the door, tiptoeing over the carpet. This is perfect: candles everywhere, duvets and blankets. I remember there is no electricity. It probably gets cold at night. I tiptoe through to the bathroom in my socks. There is a solar-panel shower, a beautiful marble basin. Everything gleams with cleanliness. As with everything so far, I should have expected the unexpected. After thinking we were going to rough it, here we are in this perfect little oasis.

Lunch is in a long dining room – heaps of glowing vegetables, silver salvers, white-coated waiters, flowers on the table. We are introduced to the owner's son. The owner is an ex-guide who founded this place a few years ago. The Americans love it. So do I; though these two days are an expensive treat. There is a lyrical peace about it. The flowers, the mountain air, the silence; a view

48

of distant, magical peaks and, nearer, high empty hills looking back at us through the windows.

I wish we could stay here forever, and didn't have a long hot walk this afternoon. Adrian has explained that we are going into Dhulikhel town, which is down the road a mile or two. We will be dropped off nearby, then this afternoon we'll walk back through the hills.

There is a history to all this. Last November, on the first of these walking holidays, a couple of women didn't want to go on the long ridge walk (that's tomorrow for us), so they set off exploring on their own and discovered a school in Dhulikhel. They were so impressed by what they saw, after spending all day there, that they came back and told everyone else about it. The people of the town are trying to build a bigger school for more pupils, and here they hope to educate the children of the Untouchables alongside the others. The caste system has been outlawed in Nepal, but still exists in reality. No one wants to sit next to the Untouchables, they are unwilling to go to school and be shunned, so they don't get educated.

The first group thought it was a worthwhile project. Everyone went back the next day, and they collected some money for the school. They actually need £10,000 – that's for a whole school. Someone in our group points out that he has just spent that on a small extension to his house.

The second group got involved in this school project, and we are being asked to do the same. Most people are enthusiastic, which is a measure of the kind of people there are in the group. Despite the white hats, the majority are genuinely interested in the country. Between us we collect well over £150, which is quite good as there only eighteen of us. It seems a better way of helping than doling out random rupees to salve our consciences.

We are walking into Dhulikhel. It is dusty and dirty on the road. We are confused by the huge buildings, which rear above us, casting long shadows. There are children everywhere. They shout at us *'Namaste! Hello! Are you English, please? I can speak English, please!'*

Two filthy little boys, with yellow-encrusted noses and ragged shirts, run up to me, shouting *'Hello!'* They want to hold my hand, but I recoil from touching them. They smile and laugh, running beside me, stretching out their grimy little hands again.

Something happens to me. I couldn't begin to find words for it. Like pain, like joy, like something sad. I stretch out my hands. The two children laugh. Tiny, cold, dirty hands are in mine. I feel ridiculous tears spring up behind my eyes.

Why am I always on the edge of crying in this place? I am reminded, at every turn, of those infinite doorways, the vision I glimpsed above Pashupatinath. How can I have so many beginnings in so short a time, again and again walking through doorways into light?

Children are everywhere, shouting and laughing. A mother holds up her baby in a bright patch of sun for me to see, another smiles and says *'Namaste!'* Smells are terrible, there are goats everywhere too, dust, and noise. Yet the world is in this place, and I reach my hands out to it, though I am still afraid. The children who ran to me had more trust.

We walk on in a confusion of life, children, chickens and goats, open-fronted shops, not at all like Kathmandu, but perhaps, like it once was. There is no traffic, just people, goats and sacred cows, the odd bicycle, once a motor cycle cutting a swathe to impress.

I am aware, with this strange new consciousness, of the sharp light and deep shadow, of eyes watching us from everywhere from these extraordinary tall buildings. There must be four or five stories to each house. And everywhere is broken stone. There was an earthquake here recently, and the town has not yet recovered. It would explain a great deal. There is a sense of riches passed away, of some great past, of people living in the ruins of it. Yet not a dying feeling, but life, all around, and always the children running beside us, laughing, leading us on.

8

By the time we reach the school, I am dazed and confused. In my mind, I want to cross the bridge. But I am still standing on the far side of the ravine, looking across. The monkeys jumped the river at Pashupatinath quite recklessly. I can't. And how can I be sure of anything?

Here is the school, like something out of a Gothic fairy tale, a witch's house, lopsided, wood-bleached to grey, silver-grained by age and weather. We stand in the tiny courtyard looking up. I can see feet through great holes in the planking. A huge crack runs from top to bottom in the wall.

We file in, uncomfortably, to view the children. I hang back till last, finding it hard to go in. The downstairs classroom has an earth floor, wooden benches crowded with children, all sizes, girls on one side, boys on the other. In the gloom the red tikka spots glow on foreheads, faces smile. Girls in white or blue shirts, boys in Coca Cola caps or the woven, softly-coloured topi hats I have seen on boys and men everywhere.

The children stand up for us in the cramped space and say in chorus *'Good Afternoon, Madam. Good Afternoon, Sir.'* It is charming, yet acutely embarrassing. I feel very unworthy.

Here, downstairs, is a male teacher in a shirt and sweater. I see books in the gloomy dimness, light only from unglazed windows. However, there is an air of order and discipline, which in my tatty classroom back in England is not always the case. The kids are doing what they're told. They are maybe even glad to be there.

Then out into the sun, everyone else standing around uncomfortably while I, last as usual, climb the rickety, gappy staircase, festooned as usual with cameras, bum bag and mini tape recorder.

In the upstairs classroom, a woman teacher in a turquoise sari smiles at us and once again we go through this ritual '*Good Afternoon, Madam, Good Afternoon, Sir,*' which so turns my heart. It is still as full of charm and spontaneity, despite the fact that I am the eighteenth visitor to come into the room in the last twenty minutes.

This is the class for the older students, though they all look very mixed in age to me. Politeness, studious faces, children eager to learn, giving up something to be here. I haven't felt that in a long time. I wonder what they would make of the school where I teach part-time, seventeen hundred students barging each other in the corridors, the odd one who sniffs correcting fluid, the odd one who blew up the boys' toilets with a fire bomb. Here in an unlit, earth-floored, hot little room, bodies jammed into a small space, there is something else.

We walk across the road in a little procession on our way to the temple. There is to be a ceremony, at which we will present the money we have collected to the town dignitaries. The temple is a pagoda structure with tiled decoration on the outside. Inside it is more like a village hall than a temple, without the plastic chairs and the WI tea urn.

There is a formal atmosphere, heavy with ceremony. I am nervous of doing the wrong thing. We take off our shoes by the door and sit cross-legged on the mats. The town dignitaries face us in a semicircle. I am desperate not to point the soles of my feet at anyone, as this is very impolite, but sitting in this unaccustomed position, with my dress over my knees, makes my thighs ache.

There is an awkward pause, during which the dignitaries look at us and smile. We look back and smile in response. There is a general atmosphere of goodwill. I suppose they are nervous too. Looking around, I see how very empty it is inside the room. We are so used to our churches being full of clutter, and of course if one looks at places like Swayambhunath, that's pretty cluttered too. But then I remember Samye Ling, the Tibetan temple in

Scotland, and how bare that was – a polished floor like our gymnasium at school, very cold on the feet, pillars and low benches and the great Buddha at one end. The walls here are painted that particular shade of green which makes it feel even more like a village hall, which I guess it is in its way. There are coloured friezes on the walls instead of playschool paintings, an iron staircase up one side.

A small man in a sleeveless fawn jumper and white shirt springs to his feet. He stands there in his socks, looking nervous, and introduces himself as Bed, which makes us smile. His English is almost perfect. He explains that he is the District Representative for Education in this area, and goes on to tell us about the town's hopes for the new school, and about how much they have raised already. One of the merchants in the town has donated £2,000. That is a staggering amount of money when one thinks about the average wage in Nepal – around £50 a month. The official indicates an elderly merchant sitting on the floor in a white topi and we all clap enthusiastically. However, even with our donations, they will still need almost £8,000 for the new building, so there's a long way to go.

Then he goes on to say how much they value contacts with England and with English schools and how such links could be beneficial to us both. He speaks about the philosophy of trying to reach all the people in Nepal with Education, especially poor and disadvantaged children. I could be in England a hundred years ago, listening to social reformers with the same eloquence and passion. I have to remind myself that he is not even speaking his native language.

I believe in this man, standing here in his knitted jumper and his socks, so slight and thin, burning with nervous energy, his glasses gleaming at us, while the town officials listen and nod. I think of my grandmother founding one of the first schools for handicapped children in England and of her reforming zeal, though she died before I was born, so I never knew her. (By all accounts she was an old dragon.) Was that how she sounded, then, burning with passion? We in the West seem so weary now, so cynical, in our tired old world. This vision of an Aristotlean future – equal opportunity, Rousseau freeing man from his chains. I've been there too. I believed in all that once, but the rawness of it went away and I became middle-aged and middle-class, and forgot.

Now here it is again. I think how disillusioned I have become with teaching since those inspiring years working with Sophie - the deaf girl I taught for four years. It was such a high when something went right. I would drive home at sixty miles an hour, singing. I haven't felt like that very often since. Now, I sit agonizingly on the floor, going down into some inner life, thinking about sea-changes. Looking up I see that Sharma is looking at me, as though once again he knows my thoughts.

Bed finishes his speech and we all clap. He looks embarrassed, as though he had been carried away by his own eloquence. He sits down, looking at the floor. There is a pause and then Adrian gets to his feet in a tangle of legs. He presents the money we have collected. He seems so huge, especially after Bed. I see the tips of his ears have gone red. He makes a graceful speech and everyone claps. They clap and we clap.

Rather breathlessly, and encouraged by the niceness of everyone, I stand up and say that my school, or maybe my youngest child's school, could set up a link with their school. I don't know what makes me say such a thing, except I know it would be good for us and perhaps it might be good for them. I suppose I too get a bit carried away by the emotion of the moment. Afterwards I am embarrassed, but everyone claps again.

A very old man appears at the top of the staircase, carrying glasses of black tea on a tin tray. He ambles down while everyone waits, and hands a glass to each of us. I know this is a great honour, but I am microbe-phobic about drinking after all I have been told, despite all my inspirational feelings of the last few moments. Out of the blue I am reminded of Prufrock.

'Shall I part my hair behind? Do I dare to eat a peach? I shall wear white flannel trousers and walk upon the beach.'

I haven't thought about that poem for years.

Gingerly I take a glass of tea, thanking the old man. Fortunately, because I am at the back, I can pretend to sip without offending anyone. If only there were an aspidistra on a corner somewhere, where I could tip it all in that time-honoured PG Wodehouse manner. I think he would have recognized the scenario. But those at the front have to drink some. Annabel and Sharma don't seem bothered anyway. Probably in a week or two, I may be like them – a wishful thought.

Kingdon-Ward, in *The Land of the Blue Poppy*, writes about his feelings on seeing the Tibetan cook rolling tsampa in his hand (roasted barley flour turned into a kind of paste by rolling it in butter tea). He notices that the tsampa is getting greyer and greyer and wonders how he will ever bring himself to eat it after seeing what the cook's hands are used for (nose wiping etc). Mind you, the left hand is reserved for defecation and doesn't handle food. Thus, you must never touch anyone with your left hand. It is a great insult, so we have been told. Anyway, after a few days on the trail Kingdon-Ward can't remember what it was he used to worry about, and he eats the tsampa with gusto. I hope I will become sufficiently inured not to worry any more about such things. One of our party is still not eating the food at all, but munching away at crisp bread in her room.

After a suitable pause, the old man comes among us with the tray, and we give the glasses back, with effusive thanks. His nails are black. I feel really mean about not drinking the tea, as though I am not being true to all my high-flown thoughts. The old man smiles and bows his head, and doesn't seem to mind. I daren't look up to see if Sharma is watching.

We get up stiffly and, bow our thanks, making our way out of the temple door and putting our boots on outside. Looking to the right, we catch sight of two young children washing our glasses in a red plastic bucket in a ditch. Several people who have drunk all their tea now look worried. I still feel bad about abusing their hospitality, and think how kind they were. I wish I were different, less afraid, less of a Prufrock. *'No! I am not Prince Hamlet, nor was meant to be.'* Oh, well.

We have a guided tour of the building works for the new school. They have got to first floor level, and everyone is very proud. I have an interesting chat with the Headmaster. He tells me that while they have room for fewer than 500 pupils at present, when the new school is completed they will be able to educate 900 or more children of poorer and low-caste families. I tell him a bit about the school I teach at two days a week (a sanitized version). I am the only person on this trip who has any contacts with schools, apart from Sylvia who is a retired primary teacher. Everyone else's kids are grown up and married.

I feel rather inferior to the Headmaster. His English is so good. He gives me his card. Then Bed comes to speak to me. He invites me to visit his own school, which is at the other end of the town. I thank him and say I will try to come, and that I am very honoured by the invitation. Bed carefully writes down his name, the name of his school and his home telephone number. He says they are very anxious for contacts with English schools. Will I please come? Sharma comes up behind me and says that he will try to arrange it. I feel I want to come back, but as with the tea half an hour ago, I am afraid. I couldn't really say what I am afraid of. It isn't microbe-phobia now. It is of crossing that bridge. Suddenly, I am outside this group of people I didn't feel entirely part of in the first place, but who made me feel secure. It is my fault for speaking up in such a foolish way about school links and all that officious stuff. I actually can't bear people who do things like that. It really isn't me and for the life of me I can't imagine why I did it. Now I've opened up a real Pandora's box...

9

We say our goodbyes and straggle along the dusty road towards the outskirts of the town. Children walk with us, touching us. Old women, squatting beside their doorways, put their hands together and smile, 'Namaste!' School is out and workers are coming back from the fields.

The streets are more crowded. We walk carefully, avoiding the splodges of unidentifiable dung, the soapy grey puddles of stinking water, the blocks of masonry lying in the road, the rubble, the goats which spring around us, running and playing just as the children do.

The goats are wonderful. There are floppy-eared kids curled asleep on the rush mats among the chickens, black, brown and pure white. I know goats, but these mixtures defy a name. The odd sacred cow browses along. We pass a Medical Centre with a blue sign in English and Nepali. It looks just like a shop, with the same dark doorway, and a woman stands outside in a pink blouse, scratching herself sleepily.

The town no longer seems sinister. I know people here now. There have been the beginnings of friendships. Walking with the light behind me, I find it full of life, and gay. There are carvings everywhere, on the black wood beside doorways, over the lintels, and on beams lying in the street. It is just as a Tudor town must have looked when it was a living place, not in a museum.

I grew up in a house with carving like this - Cardinal Wolsey's house in Ipswich, where my parents rented an ornate flat with pargetted ceilings for 15 shillings a week (75p). There was the same black wood, beautiful brick and plaster, and carved doorways, small like these, where my father (over 6 foot) was always banging his head. But of course these doorways fit the people very well, although the houses are so tall, almost out of proportion to the people-sized doorways.

These are Newari houses. The Newars were the original inhabitants of the valley, famous for their carving and beautiful silverwork. You see it everywhere on the houses and in the temples in Kathmandu. The Newari influence spread as far as China and into Tibet. This is still a town of the Newars.

The dust is choking and dry. It grits in my teeth. God knows what's in it. We are kicking it up as we stride purposefully through the town. There are some really impressive walkers in our little lot. They treat every walk as a mini-marathon and that means I am always left behind, even when I am not taking pictures, recording children singing, playing back *Good Morning/Hello/I speak English Madam* to the fascinated kids whose voices I have caught on the recorder. Trouble is, it gets a bit too popular, and I wish I hadn't started. There is also something tasteless about flashing hardware around for the benefit of the local people, although they do love to hear their voices.

Glen is also being besieged. It seems to have got round town that he has a pocketful of pens. They are crazy for pens, and very soon he has run out. Yet the children, not begrudging his lack of largesse, still run beside him and hold his hand, just because he's nice. His favourite word is Magic! and he says it all the time, entranced by the kids.

There is graffiti everywhere on the walls in English and Nepali – *Vote for Tree, Vote for Sun* – with suitable visual aids (i.e. a drawing of a stylized tree like something out of an antique tapestry, and a round sun). Sharma has said there have been elections recently. He doesn't elaborate. This is still a sensitive issue. One is not supposed to talk politics. We don't press him further.

There is a magnificent multi-coloured billy goat standing with his harem under a brick wall where *Vote for Tree* is written in red paint, with a white-painted tree beside it. He too looks like something out of an old tapestry. Only like everything in this place he isn't frozen in some other time, some Breughel-esque moment when Icarus is falling out of the sky and the peasants, uncaringly or unaware, are labouring in the fields. He is very much alive.

I am struck by how well all the animals look, except the dogs – tiny baby goats, cows, water buffaloes, even some dogs, though not the dead ones which lie in the gutter crawling with flies. Being a serious dog lover, I do find that distressing. But the dogs sleep so deeply that I find myself trying to decide whether their flanks are going up and down... or not, because flies crawl over the live ones too.

The Nepalese people do seem to look after their animals, even when they have so little themselves, though how that reverence for life squares with ritual sacrifice, I haven't yet figured out. I suppose in some mysterious way it is the other side of the coin, but I have yet to get to grips with that idea. At least the hypocrisy we so often practise in our Western religions seems to be absent. I remember my mother telling me that she had walked through Assisi, where St Francis had lived, and an Alsatian was lying in the shadow of the basilica, still alive, with its face half-eaten away. It was in agony, but everyone just walked past. Mind you, thinking about it, what could one do? We aren't so wonderful. Don't like to think about the sacrifices, though. They still go on; goats, chickens, pigeons, though I haven't seen any bloodstained shrines here so far.

A whole family is sitting outside their door, all on one rush mat – a microcosm of Nepalese life; a tiny girl in a beige linen shift, a woman in a lime green and pink sari with a green cloth over her head, a small boy in pale blue trousers and a pink shirt, asleep on a pink-shawled shoulder, an old man in a dark jacket sitting on the step, and a woman in a red sari with a black shawl, carrying a baby. All have their bare feet on the rush mat, which lies on the broken square stone cobbles in the sun, their shoes laid alongside in neat pairs.

I count eight people on the mat, with a little white goat and a brown chicken. A shaft of sunlight, cut out of the black shadow, illuminates them like an illustration from life, without the capital L. But this is not how I have seen life (with or without the capital L) till now. We smile at one another, the whole family and I, and I feel so drab in the face of all this colour. If only I had a little time to stop and sit here in the sun, just being.

Just as I am thinking again how our lives must have once been like this, our towns full of street life, Sharma comes up alongside me with his weightless step.

'Don't make the mistake of thinking this is a medieval society. It's far more complex than that.'

I don't like to say I was. I suppose it is dangerous romanticism to think in such a way. This is a very ancient, structured society, which in its own way has changed and developed quite differently from our own. In many ways - spiritually, for example - it is very sophisticated. I am caught in the trap of applying my own Western standards (again).

Sharma points to a large pink building over to the left, set back from the road.

'That's Bed's school. If you really want to go, I'll telephone him. The others are going on the very long walk tomorrow, a nine-hour ridge walk. I don't want to walk so far!' He grins at me. 'Anyway, there will be a local guide. If it is important for you to go back to the school, I will arrange it if you wish.'

The town peters out into a trail. Children from the secondary school catch up with us, books under their arms. I recognise some faces from the dim classroom. They greet us like old friends. One small boy walks beside me, silently, smiling often but saying nothing. I feel gladdened by his presence. The trail steepens into a dusty yellow, rocky, track between high banks with vegetation. The sun is still very hot. I am soon breathless and left behind. I see that the local guide we have for today (in addition to Sharma) hangs back behind me to make sure I don't get lost. I smile at him and say, 'Looking after the old lady! Thank you!'

His tells me his name is Kedar. I know he works at the Lodge where we are staying. He smiles and says, 'No hurry! Please!' I am touched by his care.

It is very hot and dry, dusty and steep. That little boy still walks lightly beside me in his flip-flops, carrying his school books. He is wearing a beige anorak and two shirts and has a satchel over his chest. He is not out of breath at all. I suppose he walks this trail every school day. I glimpse Sharma and Annabel and all the others at the bend in the trail, a hundred yards ahead; Sharma walking effortlessly in his trainers and Annabel in her white Hush Puppies. They are climbing easily up these rock steps where I am floundering, my mouth full of dust. I can see why everyone spits round here. But still Kedar walks behind me, quiet and unperturbed, leaving me to my own pace.

Will it always be like this? I thought I was pretty fit – all those winter afternoons struggling up the steep face of Carrock with the long-suffering dog, slipping on the frozen, glassy streams, stumbling through the bracken, my chest and throat aching with the cold. But they are a formidable bunch ahead, despite appearances, who walk every God-sent hour with their pedometers and their maps in plastic sleeves. This afternoon's little jamboree must seem nothing more than a stroll along the prom.

The little boy shows me his English text book. He tells me he has a two hour journey to school every day down the trail, and two hours back. I don't know if he still goes to school in the monsoon. I try to ask but we have a communication breakdown, although his English is really very good. His textbook is an old-fashioned reader, the kind I grew up with – stiff, formal sentences in big print, and little informative black and white drawings. He is very proud of it. He also shows me his English writing book. Very neat.

It is rather difficult to have these high-powered conversations about Education while I am completely out of breath, struggling up yet another rocky trail. However, we manage, though when I play my tape recorder back afterwards I don't seem to have said much except 'Good! *(pant, pant)* Very good! *(pant, pant)*' which says a great deal about non-verbal communication on both sides. We actually learn quite a lot about each other, though I do sound impossibly pompous. He doesn't seem to mind.

At last I get to the top of this particular foothill. There is a flat bit here, mercifully, where I can catch my breath. A long, long view down across the wooded foothills in the afternoon sun, folds of ochre, gold and green, a cool breeze, and the chance to gulp some iodine-flavoured water. I look round for my little friend but he has melted away, off home on his own track. I never got to grips with his name. I feel a curious sense of loss. He never asked me for a pen, or a rupee, or anything, other than that I should look at his books. It was a very equal fleeting friendship on a long hot stretch of the trail. I shan't forget him. I wonder if he will remember me.

As I puff up the next hill, a young man runs alongside me. He looks wild, desperate, and tells me he has things to sell. He shows me an amber-coloured bracelet which is carved and inlaid with silver, and a beautiful kukri (Ghurkha knife), also chased with silver. He says they are very old. I know are rules about not buying any objects of more than a certain age, and if these are as old as they look, I could get into trouble. I say I have no money. He is very persistent. The others are getting further ahead. Even my little minder has gone on a little way. I am quite alone on the trail.

I hurry on as fast as I can, trying to be courteous, but repeating all the time 'I have no money. No rupees!' He is asking a high price, but as he walks beside me, his voice becomes increasingly desperate. The price comes down dramatically. I feel sorry for him. But I daren't buy, and it is true that I have hardly any rupees on me.

We round the corner. Thank goodness, the others have

stopped.

'These people ahead. They may want to buy!' Very cowardly.

He leaves my side. I am relieved but still feel really bad. What if he is a refugee? In the end, no one buys, and he runs off. Someone says he is probably a smuggler, or the things are fake.

I manage to catch up with the others, who have stopped for a brief rest. Of course, just as I get there, they decide to go on again. Still, now it is not so steep and I can keep up a lot better. Another older boy walks with us with an even bigger pile of books under his arm.

His English is very sophisticated and he tells me what each member of his family does. His father is a farmer, like everyone in these hills, and his mother helps in the fields. It's actually the other way round from what I have seen so far, with the women doing the lion's share of the work. He is the eldest son, and his brothers and sisters are still at school. He would like to be a teacher. I wonder what chance he will stand. There is an acute shortage of trained teachers, but the logistics of sparing the eldest son from the essential work in the fields, and of raising the cash to send him down to Kathmandu, must make such dreams well-nigh impossible. Sharma tells me that graduates from Kathmandu University are expected to spend a year teaching in the hills. He himself is a Mathematics graduate. The Nepalese government is keen to get proper teacher training systems under way, but the problems are staggering.

Kedar also walks with me and tells me about his family and his work at the mountain lodge. It sounds like a good job. He waits at tables, helps out in the kitchen, and is also employed as a local guide for visitors to the lodge. Living in the hills, he knows the trails very well.

We are walking high up now on a ridge. I have no idea how high. It is surprising how quickly my breathlessness disappears. I have had no more trouble with altitude, or whatever it was that made me feel so strange this morning. We must be much higher than the mountain lodge, yet, apart from on the steep bits, I feel fine.

We can look down into the valleys, which are filling with purple shadow as evening approaches. The sun sinks lower in the sky and there is a scent of wood fires. It is indescribably lovely and peaceful. Glen and I stop by a family who are preparing their evening meal alongside the trail. He squats down with his straw hat tipped over his nose, which causes much hilarity. The woman and her daughter, or daughter-in-law, are preparing a fresh green vegetable which looks like spinach, in metal dishes on the ground, while a tiny boy plays with a black kid with white ears. He stares solemnly at us, these visitors from outer space, and although the others smile and laugh at Glen's hat, he is too puzzled by us to find it funny.

The man of the house comes out of their single-storey hut wearing a Walkman clamped to his head. He greets us, smiling, and explains, in excellent English, that he has a very good bed. His wife is nodding and smiling. He goes on to say that a beautiful lady from the United Kingdom stayed in his house last year and she said how good the bed was. Would I please recommend it to my friends in England? They may wish to come and stay. Would I like to inspect it? I look apprehensively into the dark doorway, making appreciative noises. Fortunately we are being left behind, so I have an excuse to hurry on, making promises as I go, about how I will tell all my friends. They smile and wave, all except the little boy who sits with the goat kid in his arms. Unmoving, he stares after us....

We are walking through fronded bamboo, and there is pink blossom on a bush beside the trail. Spring is beginning here, high up in the foothills, though we are too early to see the best of the flowers. But above us are the palm-like green leaves of a banana tree, with a gigantic purple flower hanging underneath. It reminds me vividly of an elephant's genitals, heaven knows why. Then, as we pass the banana tree, someone says, out of the blue, that it is Budget Day in England. Back in the UK, serious folk will be waiting with baited breath to hear whether a quarter of a penny will be knocked off income tax, and here I am thinking about banana flowers and elephants, walking down a trail in the Himalayan foothills.

We begin to descend from the ridge. I can understand why I have been warned that going down is hard on the knees and hips. Literally hundreds of stone steps, how old one can only guess. Who could have built them? A definite leg wobble begins. It is so dusty I wrap my 'yashmak' over my mouth. On and on, down the stone steps, wrapped in my own world. Coming round a corner, I am faced by a reception committee at the bottom, cameras poised. I am caught on film, a squat figure in a long skirt, hat jammed down over eyes, yashmak over nose, an invisible woman in a cloud of personal dust.

At last, as shadows spread across the path, we glimpse the thatched huts of the lodge below us in the trees. I am sweating, covered in dust, very weary, and my hips ache. As we arrive on the terrace, a group are having evening drinks. We are invited to join in. It is all rather elegant, little hors d'oeuvres, and a punch. People have just arrived -German and American- are all dressed up, the women in sparkly sweaters and long skirts. I feel dirty and scruffy and I don't like being looked down upon. It brings out all my social climbing instincts. Do we never change? I thought I might have moved on from such feelings, today.

My back is soaked in sweat, and I am beginning to chill in the evening breeze. After a sip of a drink and a couple of peanuts, I make my excuses and go off to wrestle with the solar-panelled shower. Then I sit on the wall outside, watching the sun go down, drying my hair in the evening wind. I can look down at the little farm below me, its few tiny terraced fields, children playing with the goats, the sounds of a flute wandering up to me. A man is doing some woodwork, banging away at something. Behind him are the immense, serene hills, lying lynx-like and silent in tawny shadow. And beyond,are the high Himalaya, shining down on the world. I can't see them yet, but I know they are there.

All the feelings that have come upon me today are brought together in a moment of deep peace. If this is joy, then in this moment I have it. Sitting here, on this brick wall, in the evening sun, with flowers and birdsong and mountains, I ask for nothing more.

With a little while till dinner, I wander alone in the gardens. It seems that I am seeing these flowers for the first time. Sweet peas drift in fragrant clouds of colour along the pink brick walls. Bougainvillea drapes itself around the backdrop of mountain and shadow. Not just, *I see*, more *I feel*. Even, *I am*.

The jasmine scatters a scent of evening. And something else is here, entirely new. It is as though I have been newborn in this mountain kingdom. I am all spirit and peace. It doesn't matter how silly and muddled and foolish I am. I have something here I will never lose, nor ever forget....

There are shining faces in the candlelight at a long table. The mountains are out there, in the dark. An eternal, powerful presence. Neither frightening nor benign. After dinner I am escorted back to my hut by an old gardener who carefully holds a lamp in front of me so that I do not trip on the shallow steps. I thank him and say *'Namaste!'* and he bows away into the night. I fumble about for my head torch, then light a candle on the little table. I sit alone in my room, not lonely, looking out of the wide window onto the unseen mountain.

Later I walk out and sit on the wall, breathing the silence. The fires still glow, small spots of light flickering in the greater darkness of the hills. A truck whines its way up the Tibet road below me, its headlights briefly illuminating the dry trees. Then all is quiet again. A thin crescent moon lies on its back.

Back in my own room, the darkness is deep. I light the little candles in their candlesticks – real candlesticks crafted by someone who loved these little objects, a Tibetan craftsman. But the candlelight is hardly enough to go round the room. I sit against the window and write a letter home, guilty that I have not felt more guilty, but I have been so full of joy. I should have missed them more.

10

We are in a grassy meadow. Most of the group are standing on a knoll pointing their cameras to the east. Children come and stand beside us, and together we look over the folds of grey insubstantial hills, towards a faintly lit sky. It is cool and fresh, and the first birds are singing in the valley.

Everyone is very quiet, even reverential. The trees are black silhouettes, and there is a sense of waiting, a tension broken only by spitting from the children. I take off most of my layers, down to a short-sleeved shirt, placing my three cameras on the grass. I have a Pentax, an Olympus automatic which I use most of the time, and a disposable panoramic camera which takes three pictures in line. It will only do twelve shots but it seemed worth buying for such a special experience. Unfortunately, as we wait in the breathlessness quiet, I have to get Glen to read out the instructions on the side, as I have forgotten my glasses.

There does seem to be a real drawback. We can see plenty of high ridges and foothills which vanish into the distance in a linear wash of dawn light, but in the pearly sky over to the east, there is a distinct lack of mountains. Nevertheless, we gaze on, full of anticipation, hoping those peaks will pop up with the sun like a backdrop in *Swan Lake*.

They don't.

The sun blips shyly over the rim of the last ridge. As it climbs into the sky, the whole valley below is touched by colour, the sky turning brilliant pink and orange, a new beginning of the world. We take lots of pictures of foothills and the sun rising and trees in silhouette, but there are no snowy peaks. For someone, somewhere, the first rays lights them to fire. But not for us, not just yet.

Nevertheless, I am glad, with morning gladness, that I am here. I like the valleys and the shadows, the world coming alive, birds singing their hearts out luminously with the first touch of the sun, the freshness and excitement. A hundred times over, it was worth getting up for, climbing here to see the sun over these endless valleys. I don't really like the hawking and spitting (nothing's perfect) but I really don't mind so much about not seeing the high mountains (though if I had, I would probably change my mind). Glen says it is because of the dust haze. But some part of me thinks it is just not time. And there is always tomorrow, our last day in Dhulikhel.

It has been agreed that I will walk the first few miles with the others, then go back with Sharma, who will take me to the school. It is very hot, even this early. I am still puffing and panting, but keeping up better. The last few days of walking five or six hours a day have begun to make a difference. I already feel fitter, even without much sleep....

We climb the first part of the trail, narrow dusty paths, quite high up, where there is only room to put one foot in front of the other. Heaven knows how the people manage with those huge baskets on their backs.

There are little ochre houses, beehive-shaped haystacks hanging like giant nests from the trees, calves and goats flicking their ears in their thatched shelters – an air of peace and harmony. I rather wish I were going on, though I don't fancy a long day with no shade, walking along a ridge.

We say goodbye to the others. Sharma and I walk shyly together down the trail. A girl of about eight has been walking ahead of us for a while, and now she turns back to walk beside us. She has her hair in bunches, and tells me she is on her way to school. School starts at 10a.m., so she is already late. Sharma is asking her questions. She nods and points over to the right. Then he stops and explains that there is a famous holy man -a sadhu- who lives close to this trail, but Sharma has never found the sanctuary where he lives. Would it be OK if we try to find him together?

I am fascinated, but a bit apprehensive. What about the school? Sharma says that when we have found the sadhu (if we do) we will walk down to the village where the bus will be waiting for us. There is a telephone there. He will phone the school and say that we are coming.

We turn off the main trail and walk along a pale sandy track which climbs again. It is really hot now. I wonder how long we will have to walk, even though I really want to see the sadhu. I hope he won't mind my coming, but I somehow instinctively know that Sharma will look after me. I feel completely safe with him. Strange, as I have known him for such a short time.

He guides me down the path, helping me over the steep rocky bits. The little girl walks ahead and then calls out '*Namaste*', disappearing down another path. We walk on for quite a long time. It is really wild here, and we only pass one or two little huts, then nothing, just open scrubland and rock. It's very quiet.

Suddenly we are under trees in deep, sun-dappled, shady woodland. We cross a little stream beside a hill. Pine trees are growing thickly on the slopes. It is silent and cool. We walk on and on through fallen pine needles, thick underfoot. There are small blue flowers growing by mossy stones. It reminds me a little of the Suffolk breckland where I grew up. I have felt the same mystery of the deep woods, standing in Tunstall Forest watching the sun's rays slanting down – the sandy soil, that same sharp scent of pines. There is no wind here, no exciting sense of the distant sea. Yet there is something else. Some calm. Some feeling of the spirit. As powerful here as anywhere I have ever been.

The path leads us downwards. Then, in a little clearing, a natural bowl on the side of the hill, we see white buildings through the trees. We walk down. There is a stone tank with water flowing into it, flowers and trees, a white shrine and a small white house. Beyond, a view over the hills.

A girl swathed in orange cloths and wearing a turban is

squatting by running water, washing a shiny pot over and over till it gleams. She looks up and smiles. Although she is quite brown, I am sure she is European. She has colouring like mine, although I can only see a few strands of her hair.

Sharma speaks to her in Nepali (I suppose) and she answers. Then in perfect, accented English she says, 'It is OK for you to go inside. My sadhu is there. He will see you.'

I feel as though nothing that happens here is strange. That is the strangest thing. I am wearing my 'yashmak', and I pull it up to cover my head. There is a sort of gateway, not with walls on either side, just set in air, so you could walk round if you wanted. But we walk through, taking off our shoes. I am quite timid; not afraid, just not wanting to do the wrong thing. There are flowers in the sun, the sound of water running into the stone tank, lotus flowers growing on the water, the shining white of the stone shrine.

Inside is a garden and the little temple, open on all sides, like the Shiva lingam shrines at Pashupatinath. And inside here too is a lingam, painted red and yellow. We stand beside the little shrine for a few moments in the intense quiet, feeling the sun on us. Actually, there are birds singing and that sound of the water, but it doesn't affect the silence.

Then we walk quietly to the place where the girl has laid out mats on the ground. We sit facing the little house. The door is closed. There is a sort of clay altar in front of the steps, flat with a low clay wall all around and all sorts of objects on it. Fruit, dried herbs, offerings. In the middle of the flat altar is a huge conical pile of smouldering ash, with a thin line of smoke rising; a scent of herbs.

Suddenly, the sadhu is here. He is very tall, dressed in an old sweater (the sort you might buy in the Lake District) and an orange sarong. He is quite fearsome, his face covered with ash and white paint, his hair so long it spreads over the ground in snake-like ropes. His beard is all shades of yellow-white and grey and grows down across his chest, tied in a big knot above his waist.

Apart from all these extraordinary things his eyes are mesmerising, outlined in black, glowing at me out of his ash-white face, almost angrily. Perhaps I am right to be scared. But Sharma is sitting beside me, serenely, in the lotus position. I feel that nothing that happens can be really bad. In fact I am *awestruck* more than frightened. That is the only word for it – awestruck by the place, by the sense of it, by the absolute feeling of holiness, by this magnetic, magical, powerful figure in front of me.

The sadhu squats down by his fire and says some prayers. I don't know how I know they are prayers, but I do. I look at Sharma and he looks at me and smiles his wonderful smile, as though all of this were the most natural thing in the world.

The sadhu puts a handful of herbs on the fire. He looks at Sharma and starts to speak. Sharma then opens a little pocket book, consults it and begins to ask questions. They have a brisk exchange in which the sadhu seems to be telling him off. I hope he isn't getting into trouble for bringing me. But Sharma doesn't seem at all discomforted. He smiles and shakes his head. Then he turns to me and says,

'The sadhu is rebuking me. He says if I want to know the answers to these deep questions I must stay for three days, but I have told him we have to go soon. He is rather cross.'

The sadhu starts up again, ranting at Sharma. While he is speaking, the girl, who is sitting watching me, speaks to me in English. She tells me she is a 'gita' (pupil). She came from Belgium 'some time ago'. She looks after the sadhu and learns from him. She tells me that together they made this place. There was nothing here, only the water. They have cleared the scrub and fertilised the soil to make a sanctuary, planted flowers and new trees. While they were clearing the land they found an old stone lingam buried in the ground. So this had been a holy place before. Now the lingam is in the shrine.

I seem to have stepped through yet another doorway into a place where these things are true, and taken for granted. And I too, at this moment, have no trouble in knowing that they are indeed true. I know these things with another part of me, which I have hardly been aware of till now; with another sense which I have used and known about, yet never believed. The sense I used when I walked in the breckland forest and felt things I couldn't explain, the sense I have keyed into, almost with an audible click, an awareness of something, for which there is quite simply no word in my language. *Otherness.* That is about the closest I can get. I wouldn't mind betting that Nepali and Newari, Hindi and Tibetan, and all the Eastern languages, have perfect words for this. But here I am, floundering like a non-swimmer in deep water, because I have never been taught the strokes.

How odd. Here I sit, on this rush mat, listening to a philo- sophical dispute between Sharma and the holy man, without understanding a word, talking a little to the gita, yet I am not out of my element. I just don't have words, or the experience. New feelings are coming up inside me, but they feel like very old ones. And bubbling up from somewhere is a feeling like memory, as though I knew all this once, and then forgot.

The sadhu is angry again. He waves his arms wildly and shouts. I wonder if he has just made some great pronouncement. But Sharma is laughing. The girl smiles and shakes her head.

'He is always angry with the village women. They come and wash their clothes in our water tank. It pollutes the water, and besides, it is holy.'

The sadhu begins to walk clockwise round the clay altar, intoning prayers. He picks up a bunch of grapes from the wall, and says a prayer over them. Then, gently, he holds out his hands to us, the black grapes cupped in his palm. I look into his fathomless eyes.

'He has blessed the grapes for us. It is a great honour. We must eat!' Sharma says, under his breath.

I smile at the sadhu, and put my hands together in an instinctive gesture of thanks, moved and touched by the ceremony, but my mind racing ahead in panic. One of the absolute rules we have been told over and over again is, *'Peel it, cook it, or forget it.'* Unwashed fruit is very dangerous. But I can hardly sit here and peel my grapes, while the sadhu intones prayers over us.

Sharma hands me the bunch, cupped in his hands as the old man has done. I know that if I don't eat, I will be insulting the sadhu and the gita, their religion, the place and all its holy feelings. Another bridge to cross, although no-one else would even guess that here I am, agonising. I smile, and take a grape, and eat. What a small thing, it seems. Yet for me with all my worries, it is another huge step forward onto the swaying planks, over the ravine.

The old man seems pleased that I have taken part in his ceremony, and I am conscious of the honour of it, despite my fears about the grapes. He says more prayers, squatting beside the altar, throwing dried flowers and herbs onto the grey smoking ash of the fire. He seems to have forgotten us.

Looking past him, through the doorway of the hut, I notice with astonishment that there is a big clock on the wall, the sort you might have in a village school, I suppose battery-operated. I can see into the little house – rugs and a table, shining clean, almost European.

Sharma whispers to me, 'We can go now, if you are ready.'

I get up as decently as I can with my stiff legs. The sadhu is far away in another world. We murmur our thanks, putting our hands together. I leave some rupees as an offering along the wall. The gita smiles at us. I think what a strong calm face she has, and wonder about her life here.

'There is so much I would like to ask you. How did you come to be here?'

She shakes her head.

'Don't talk about the past. It is another life. But yes, we will talk. When you come next time.'

I begin to explain that we leave this part of Nepal tomorrow. I will never come back. She looks at me and shakes her head again.

'You will come to Nepal again,' she says. 'Many times. And then we will talk.'

I feel there is a curious bond between us; some understanding. In that moment, I know that she is right. I will come back. That is the most mysterious thing.

We thank her, and walk out through the gateway. We put on our shoes, and I take a last look back into the inner sanctuary. The girl is standing watching us. Suddenly, in the quiet, I hear a terrible sound coming from somewhere beyond the hut. A high-pitched scream which makes my blood run cold. I have a momentary vision of some dreadful sacrificial rite.

'What on earth is that?' I ask, shaken. The girl lifts her head and listens.

'Oh! My pressure cooker! I'd forgotten all about it. I'm cooking the vegetables. I must go!' She rushes into the hut.

We walk away together up the path, away from the sanctuary, Sharma beside me with his light step. For a while I am too overcome to speak. But soon, quietly we begin to talk, Sharma and I, about our beliefs. He tells me that, although he is a Buddhist, he feels it necessary to explore all faiths, and take from each whatever wisdom he can. He talks to me about the 'Dharma', which is the Buddhist 'Way' or Teaching for Life.

'For me, the Dharma should not be a still thing like a stagnant pool, never moving nor changing. It should be as a clear running stream, giving refreshment to the spirit, open to all new ideas. All streams lead to the Dharma.'

I know that Nepalese religions show great tolerance, that Hindu and Buddhist ideas intermingle, and that their ideas of a Universal spiritual power have much in common. And in that moment, listening to Sharma's quiet voice, it seems to me that this is a way forward for all of us.

I have lived a long time in the sanctuary. What I learned there, how I began to understand so much that is unspoken, will be with me for ever. With the curious insight that this time has brought me, I see my own search, and all its small struggles, in a new light.

We talk on, sharing ideas as friends. Sharma tells me that he was a Mathematics teacher for ten years after university. He has also spent some time in a Buddhist monastery as a child. He will probably return to the monastery when his children are grown, just for a while. But now he is working as a guide to help put his children (a boy and a girl) through private schools, and he hopes to send his son to England to be a doctor. We tell each other a little about our lives.

We are out of the wooded area and on the old trail where we walked this morning. It seems that I have been a whole day in the sanctuary, days even, yet it is still not lunchtime. As so often here, time is different. We walk on down to the village, still talking. There is a little hotel in the centre. Sharma finds me a place to sit while he goes off to use the telephone. I rest in the sun looking over the foothills, pale tan and green without shadow. It is very hot again and the sun beats down on my head. I am glad I am not up there on the ridge walk. What I have seen today will be with me for ever.

Sharma comes back from the telephone, and says it is OK to go to the school. We walk into the square to find the bus driver. This takes a bit of time as he has gone off somewhere, but at last, with me ensconced like some memsahib in the exact centre of the coach (Sharma at the front), I am driven down the twisting precipitous road to Dhulikhel.

11

It could be my inner city school in the lunch hour. What's different? The girls are beautiful and dark; long hair in one immaculate plait, green shirts which look newly-ironed. Considering that many have walked two hours or more down the trail from a single-storey hut without electricity, their smart turn-out is amazing. I wonder what they would think of our precocious, slouch-socked, micro-skirted, crinkle-permed fifteen year olds who charge about the corridors, clutching shocking pink and green roll bags full of books, screaming at one another.

They all smile at me (a universal form of communication), this odd-looking woman with her safari hat and Leki stick, coming in through the gate with Sharma.

Otherwise the immediate differences from my school are that it's hot and sandy in the playground and that there are a few more holes in the walls, though not that many more. My English school is in terminal decay after years of government cuts and in one of the classrooms the ceiling is falling down.

Generally, though, because this is not the school down the road which has to be rebuilt, but Bed's own school where he teaches (the prestigious Sanjiwani High School) it is in good repair. There is no litter. At my school you can't walk from Middle to Upper School on a windy day without being hit by an empty fag packet.

We climb to the upper storey. I am unnerved by the holes in the floor of the outside walkway. Several large students are jumping up and down energetically on the single plank. Others are rushing about like kids everywhere in the lunch hour.

We are ushered into the Headmaster's office, large and cool, lots of books and several chairs with the stuffing coming out (quite like home). It has that intimidating air of a Headmaster's study anywhere.

The Headmaster rises to greet us. An impressive man, white-haired, wearing a topi. He has wonderful English and is very courteous. We shake hands. Sharma gives him two copies of *The New Scientist* which Annabel has saved for him.

He tells me he spent a year at Oxford, and we launch into a long discussion about educational needs. Once again I feel an awesome level of scholarship. Much is expected of me. I have had the cream of English education and all the chances in the world.

Bed comes in. Sharma tells me that Bed was once a pupil at this school. I ask if he was ever in trouble when he was young. The joke falls flat. They are expecting me to be more serious. Only Sharma laughs.

We talk some more, about education in Nepal, and about the problems schools face in a 'developing' country. It is hard to reach the children in the hill villages, yet the school is the crucial centre of change and development.

There is a pause while an older boy, who has been waiting outside the door, is summoned in. Tall for a Nepalese lad, he stands in front of the Head, wearing that bored, insolent expression which some members of my Year 9 English group would instantly recognize. I am rather surprised to see it here, where the young people are much more strictly brought up, and expected to do as they are told. Rather as the sadhu tore a strip off Sharma (though Sharma didn't sulk), so the headmaster does the same with this boy, who does. He retaliates once or twice and then subsides under this flood of eloquence.

It must be very hard to discipline a boy of fifteen who would normally be out in the world. In this country he could be a father of children, tilling his family's land, particularly now under the Land Acts, which in the last few years has returned some of the land to the peasants so that they have increasing autonomy.

Yet this, maybe, is only an extreme form of what we face in English schools, where sexual maturity and a desire to be out there, getting and spending in an adult world, are powerful pressures working against a young man who might want to stay on and study. How much more pressure here, in this subsistence economy, where there are such sacrifices involved in staying on to secondary education (which has to be paid for by the family) and social pressures to take one's place in the working world.

Heaven knows how any of the girls manage. It is hard enough for them to get any education anyway, as they are still seen only as homemakers. The overall literacy rate in Nepal is estimated at 34 per cent but the female literacy rate is as low as 12 per cent. (These are 1996 figures. Things have improved a bit since then.) Yet this is in a society which I find so attractive just because of the serenity and stability provided by traditional role-playing! I wonder how I would react if I had to pound clothes on a stone in the river each day? I find it hard enough to tear myself away from my books to fill up the washing machine.

Nonetheless, everyone seems to see Education as tremendously important. The care with which the girls are dressed for school, the way everyone wants to practise their English and show you their books, bear witness to that.

The boy leaves the room to join his mates, who have been waiting out of sight, giggling. I am dying to know what he has done, but daren't ask. We resume our conversation. This Headmaster impresses me more than anyone I have met in Nepal, even Bed and Sharma. I feel the weight of scholarship in his quiet manner. I hope he won't ask me anything tricky about the English novel or the development of modern poetry. I have been stealing a quick look at his bookshelves. His reading is eclectic, if his books are anything to go by. Most of the books are in English.

I have read that not many of the teachers in the hills are well-trained, except those graduates from Kathmandu who have to spend a year teaching in the hills, like Sharma. But here in this school, if the Headmaster and Bed are typical, it's a different story. Mind you, I am beginning to learn that Dhulikhel is an important place. It is the district headquarters and there are government offices here. It even has a jail. So I guess the high school will be quite important in its own right, and the centre for forward-looking ideas.

I say goodbye and shake hands, glad to have met this man. We cross the wooden walkway to Bed's office, which is mildly chaotic in a comforting way. He is obviously flustered by our presence. He wants to show me so much, and talks nineteen to the dozen, buzzing about in the cramped space like a bee in a jar. Through the gaps in the wooden walls, I can hear the sounds of children singing a playground chant. A warm wind blows through the cracks in the wooden walls with that indefinable smell of Nepal.

Every cupboard Bed opens is bulging with stuff. Things fall out all over the place. He is talking all the time, a complete contrast to the quiet headmaster. I feel they are both visionaries in their own way.

Bed talks. I listen. In fifteen minutes we cover women's Education, Community Health, the teaching of English, Environmental Education, the needs of teacher training, etc. etc.

Women's Health Education is vital if birth control and immunization programmes are to have any real impact on the hill communities. Bed tells me that a few years ago they had a fortnight's Health Education programme for women run by a visiting nurse. Since then, with a knock-on effect, thousands of women have been reached throughout the extended community (which, if you ironed out all the folds in all the hills, would be hundreds of square miles). Such a small input, such a huge effect.

Bed tells me they are desperate to set up links with the English schools for the teaching of English, and that in order to set up a proper Environmental Education project, they need the expertise we have in the West. As my sister is a Head Teacher, much involved in an Environmental Education group, I offer to put them in touch. He is overwhelmed and there follows a polite tussle about who should write first. I say it has to be him, asking for what he needs. I assure him she will write back. I promise I will not forget to tell her to expect a letter, which is what worries him. I wonder if he will ever pluck up the courage.

It seems to me that we have to listen to what the Nepalese want from us. There are such acute needs, but the people are keen to do so much for themselves that a small amount of help will work wonders. Bed explains how mis-targeting can so waste resources. Two years ago the American Cultural Center sent the school a whole English language programme, books, records, the lot. Unfortunately, the school doesn't have a record player and can't afford one. And without the 'listening' input, the programme is useless. He keeps trying to find someone who would take the records away and transfer them onto tapes (the school *does* have a tape recorder – this was before CD's were widely available).

It astonishes me that such a simple thing would be so difficult to do, but then I don't live in Nepal. Bed explains that several visitors to the school have 'promised' to do this for them, but no one actually has. So we arrange that I will take the records back to the UK and get them back here somehow. Sharma offers to bring them up to Dhulikhel.

Bed now spends some time looking for the records, which in despair, he has filed away at the back of a cupboard, but the bell rings while books are still all over the floor. It is the end of the lunch hour and he has to teach. We say goodbye and agree that he will send the records down to my hotel in Kathmandu, so that they will be there for me to collect at the end of my stay in Nepal.

We shake hands. I have made a lot of promises. The weight of them sits heavily on me. What have I done? They have so few lifelines, and are so anxious for help. I mustn't let them down.*

* *Two months later, the tapes are back in place at Sanjiwani High School. Bed comes to the UK on an educational visit and stays with us, and others in the community. A long-term link begins with my daughter Harriet's school.*

12

Sharma and I are walking down the lower trail back to the lodge, as it weaves through the gentle countryside. Banana trees and bamboo give way to soft woodland, dappled with shade. There are spring leaves, banks of grass where goats browse, thin white stems of trees with a crown of branches far above. Quiet walking, past the ochre huts sleeping in the early afternoon.

We discover a common taste in poetry, especially Wordsworth. I tell Sharma about Rydal Water and show him the picture I carry of the family standing by the lake, with the shadow of the Lion and Lamb behind; Wordsworth country. He knows his Wordsworth at least as well as I do. We quote bits to one another as we amble down the trail. Yet another strange thing, to be walking here, talking about Wordsworth.

We pass a thatched hut with a conical haystack as big as the hut beside it. A tiny boy runs out, naked except for a cloth around his middle, very brown, with a fat tummy. He stares at me with great brown eyes. Then, running away, he comes back carrying a yellow flower between finger and thumb. Gravely, he stretches out his hand and gives it to me. I take the flower and thank him, my eyes filling with tears. Overcome with shyness, he scampers away, to watch us from a safe distance. I carry the flower in my hand for a while, and then place it tenderly in my bag, meaning to keep it for ever. Sharma, watching, smiles his peaceful smile.

We walk on. It isn't too steep, and we don't hurry. Sometimes I just stand, listening to that invisible bulbul bird painting the landscape with water. Sharma pauses too, not hurried by time or targets. I catch him leaning on my Leki stick, which I have put down and forgotten yet again. He is deep in thought, looking up at the sky.

The trail runs downwards into a little valley. We find

ourselves in deep shade. There is the sound of laughter, some bellowing and crashing about. Startled, I look up and see there are cows feeding from young leaves on the steep slope above us. Half-hidden in the dimness, is a well in a stone courtyard, not near any houses. Three women are filling their pots. They have blended so well into the dappled green shade, I only notice them as we come close. They giggle at us, and, when I ask if I may take their picture, explode with laughter.

There is a shrine here, very old, covered in moss, the features quite worn away so that I can't see which god it is. The women are leaning on the white stone in the shade. They have cloths wrapped around their middles, short tops so that their bare brown midriffs are exposed, and bare feet. When I thank them for letting me take their picture – this strange woman with her hat and her tangle of cameras – they repeat my words 'Thaankyoo, thaaank-yoo'. The words echo round the shady place, ringing in the stone, not mocking; joyful. We can hear them long after we have left.

After a few miles we stop and sit on a bank. I get out my Walking magazine free gift sponge-mat-for-sitting-on which makes Sharma laugh. I still haven't crossed that many bridges. Sharma has no water with him, or any food, and it is long past lunchtime. So he and I share the last of my ginger nut biscuits and some water in one of my Woolworths plastic beakers. I wonder what he thinks about the iodine flavour. He is too polite to comment.

It's quiet and peaceful. We sit in companionable silence and I get out my flower to look at. It has already wilted, and some of the petals have fallen. There is no way I can save it as it was, except in my mind. There it is perfect and will be forever.

I am just reflecting how far we are from anywhere, when there are shouts above us. Among the tall-stemmed trees, a herd of brown and black goats are rampaging among the bushes. Three children are climbing up the bank, shouting at them. They must have been playing and forgotten about their charges. The goats are certainly up to no good. Ignoring the children, they concentrate on putting their hooves up, pulling down branches before skittering off across the bank, kicking their heels in disdain. I ask Sharma whether we shouldn't do something to help, but he only smiles and says they will come back when they are ready. I am more doubtful about this. My own goats at home like nothing better than to go walkabout, escaping down the river to our neighbour's farm, and eating all the daffodils in his garden.

We finish our biscuits and walk on, talking. I reflect that this countryside is never empty or uninhabited. There is always a hut or goats, or a woman with a *doko* full of leaves walking down the trail, or a child coming from nowhere; a loosely woven tapestry in which all things are worked in harmony. Yet this is not a perfect simile, because the picture moves and changes while seeming to be still – trees, flowers, birdsong, people and huts, with the trail as the thread that binds them. It would be hard to play that game here … animal, vegetable, or mineral, animate or inanimate. In some curious way all these things seem to exist together, and it is hard to say this is *just* a flower, or a hut, a piece of rock, or a bird. Somehow each reality seems to overflow, blur, melting into another.

I think of the documentary about Sir John Hunt's sirdar on the 1953 Everest Expedition. He was trying to explain how he felt about the mountains, and how different it was for the Sherpas than for other mountaineers. He said, *'We are the blood and the mountains are our bones'*. That's how it is. I tell Sharma about it. We have a discussion about the Nature of Reality and how the Buddhists see all things as transient; hence the Buddha's words about Suffering. How we hang onto things, not wanting them to change, decay or 'pass away'. Which of course they will. Thus, our attachment inevitably causes suffering....

We get back to the lodge mid-afternoon. Sharma asks if it is too late for lunch, but it is OK. I am hungry, hot and dusty. I make my excuses and rush off to my room for a record-breaking, thirty second shower and change of clothes, not wanting to sit down so dirty. I put on my navy floaty dress.

We sit out on the terrace, looking over the foothills, in the shade of a jasmine tree. A brilliant blue sunbird hovers, with its beak in the scarlet bougainvillea flowers. There is that song of the bulbul creating coolness. A warm breeze blows up from the valley. The jasmine tree showers tiny, yellow-scented trumpets all over the snow-white tablecloth. We eat prawns in little packages of batter like the mermaid's purses you find on the seashore, and spring onions and rice. The jasmine blossoms fall on our food, but it doesn't seem to matter. We talk of astrology and birthstones, magic and poetry. I am very happy.

At five o'clock the first scarlet-faced walkers return, telling of old campaigns, blistering heat, steep ascents and miles walked. They are satisfied with achieving so much. I am pleased for them, but I would not have given up the sadhu and the little boy with the yellow flower, the sunbird and the jasmine, for anything in the world.

The Lord giveth and the Lord taketh away. Halfway through our evening meal, just as I have been boasting about how this climate suits me and how fit I feel (fool!), I am struck down. In ten seconds I go from being wonderfully well to really ill. I can hardly find my way out of the door.

There, standing in the dark, is the kindly old man with the paraffin lamp, waiting to lead me back to my hut. But his very slowness almost spells disaster. I cannot hurt his feelings by asking him to hurry, but I only just make it in time. A white face in the shadowy mirror. Pain and unnamed fears. I huddle for warmth in my comforting sleeping bag. Was it the 'holy grape' after all? Who knows?

Sharma had told me over lunch that there will be a 'dreadful' nine hour bus journey to the West tomorrow. How will I get through? I take four Imodium in three hours. Most of all I am thankful I didn't leave the spare loo roll back in Kathmandu.

At 2 a.m. I give up the unequal struggle. I may as well pack by torchlight for the morning, and write my letter home. Here, alone on the mountainside, running out of loo roll, shivering in a cold candlelit room, I am overcome by waves of homesickness. I must have been mad to come.

The journey is every bit as bad as we think it will be. The only good thing is I am so dehydrated I don't have to get out at all, except to stretch my legs. I look up the glowing description of this journey on our itinerary, *'The drive will take you through stunning scenery of waterfalls, rice fields, valleys and villages.'* Travel agent's hype again. Why is it that the good bits are never the ones they describe, almost as though Nepal defies packaging? But yes, it is hilly, very hilly and the 'road' follows every contour and bump. We look down and see dead buses at the bottom of the valley, wheels in the air, becoming almost immune to the sight.

I sit behind Clive who is lecturing Mavis without pausing for breath, hour after hour. I fantasise about killing him. He and I share a window, and he wants it shut while I want it open (the fans in the bus don't work). Every time a truck goes past we have to shut the window quickly, or we are engulfed in clouds of choking dust. As on the journey up from Kathmandu to Dhulikhel, it's better not to look forward. The sight of trucks bearing down on us is so very unsettling. As for 'waterfalls', it's so dry you can hear the leaves crackle, if it weren't for the noise of the front axle screaming under the strain.

A lot of the time we *don't* move or only very slowly, as the section in front is being built/rebuilt while we wait in line. There are Chinese workmen, and, oddly, a British surveyor in charge. The yellow dust comes up to our axles. Thank God I don't have to get out to squat. There is just a bare rock wall, the dust and ten trucks waiting in line. Not much privacy, even if everyone on our bus looked the other way.

The bulldozers work on ahead of us. We sweat in the stifling heat. Then we lurch on a little way, the bus at times balancing half on hardcore, half up the bank beside the road, tilting over at an impossible angle. Whatever else, this is some driver. I just hope the tyres hold up, especially on the precipitous bits.

At one point we can look back and see the last section of the road twirling above the valley like a piece of string. There is a wonderful river below, the Trisuli, turquoise and clear, with little islands. The white sandy shores on the far side have that mysterious quality of places on the other bank. I stare at the view hungrily as we vibrate our stifling way through the dried-up countryside.

The stunning scenery is probably better in November, after the rains, though there will be landslides then. Just now, apart from the dry trees and the sand-coloured hills, the only colour is in the vivid red of the kapok flowers which appear attached to a totally dead tree. The tree looks as though someone had stuck crimson plastic decoration onto a piece of driftwood, something you might buy from a Christmas Fair. Yet these are real flowers, and leaves will come later, like almond blossom, with the same impression of life springing from dead wood.

Here we see the first real signs of deforestation; stumps of trees with their tops and branches lopped off for fuel, terraces smudged away by landfall. In places there is no more than a featureless blur of soil, littered with broken corpses of trees which have fallen down the mountainside.

We stop at a trucker's tea house, the Nepalese equivalent of a transport café, with a noisome loo which reduces me to breathing through a Germolene wipe. I don't fancy anything but a bottle of Coke. Sharma and Annabel are braver, each standing up by the stall with a tin plate of *daal* and rice, Annabel still cool despite the dust.

We climb back onto the road, and begin that mind-numbing, bone-aching, dust-ridden journey all over again. And we have only been travelling for two and a half hours. At times it is like sitting on a pneumatic drill. But at least at those moments we *are* moving. Sitting in the queue waiting for the next load of hardcore to be spread, going nowhere, is worse. I never thought I would say this, but thank God we are flying back, although we have just been told that if the weather is bad we may have to go through this again. Don't think I can stand it.

Just when everything seems too unbearable, Sue (my new friend) leans over to me with a note and a little carrier bag. I open the note. It says:

'Today is my birthday. Would you share it with me? Inside this bag are a few of my presents and cards. Help yourself to the perfume. It's rather special!'

I smile across at her, and mouth through the engine noise, 'Happy Birthday!' What a way to spend it!

Suddenly nothing seems so bad any more. There are foreign cards with pale roses and violets, messages in Italian and Russian, a whiff of exotic perfume, a silk scarf – feminine, exquisite gifts. Here, in dust and discomfort, these little things, transient though they may be, restore my shattered spirits.

We stop for lunch and here there are gardens, flowers and water, an oasis of green. The flowers glow for me with some special intensity, after the deprivation of the last few hours travelling through the bleached landscape. The restaurant is crowded with Chinese workers. Someone says, *sotto voce*, 'If the Chinese were building a road into my country, I would be really worried.'

Perversely, despite the journey, I am beginning to feel a lot better, and I even risk a bowl of delicious Chinese-style clear soup and buy another bottle of water. Hope I won't regret this. Some of the others are looking really ill.

We lurch on and on down the endless road. I try to sleep, but sleep, reading or any activity to pass the time, is impossible. One just has to retreat within oneself, into a dream. I see that Sharma has done just that, in the front seat.

We come to a halt again on a straight stretch of road above a deep valley, scattered with broken trees. There are buses and trucks waiting ahead of us. Men stand about and the driver holds a conversation out of the window. Word comes back to us that a child has been killed by a truck. Eventually we crawl past the spot, and I cannot help but look. There is a small girl lying very still beside the road, her black hair grey in the dust. A woman squats beside her, and further on a man is walking about, head bowed, with two others, their arms around his shoulders. We crawl past, and the image of the little girl stays in my mind, with those grave faces. For two miles further on we see people running back to the place, in ones and twos, as though they have just been told. I feel the pain of it, having children of my own, always dreading such things.

Everyone is very quiet for a while. I stare out of the window at the drop down to the riverbed, with its debris, broken tyres and stones, litter and bits of road which have come away from the edge. Not long before this child was born, this road was no more than a track. Now changes bring prosperity, new life to the hills, if it were needed. Why then does this road, even as it is being constructed before our eyes, feel like a destruction? Even before this death.

The bus climbs up and up, and then we stop again to stretch our legs and cool the bus down. For some reason the endless lines of trucks have left us and it is much quieter here. The countryside looks different, subtropical with red soil, palms, lots of bamboo. Water buffalo with calves are browsing by the side of the road.

I am startled by a loud rumbling emerging from behind a bush, like a pile of large stones sliding down a hillside. It is followed by a hawking/spitting noise, as a tiny man emerges from behind the bushes. He gives another throat-clearing demonstration (unbelievably, that was the avalanche), followed by another mega-spit, stares at us curiously for a few moments, then ambles away, waving a branch and calling to his charges. They lift their heads and consider us with dark, liquid eyes. I don't like the look of those horns. Then they amble away with the same gait as the old man, showing their hip bones.

It is getting towards evening before we labour up the last climb, descend the last mountainous section, and find ourselves in a broad river valley surrounded by terraced hills. I am catatonic with tiredness, bruised by the constant lurching of the bus, sweaty and dusty, but we all feel a certain euphoria at not having gone over the side of a cliff. However, as we drive through the outskirts of Pokhara, the feeling of anticipation disappears. This seems to be a real shanty town, and in retrospect, the outskirts of Kathmandu didn't seem so bad. There are shacks and tin roofs. People stand about listlessly in the dusty evening light. Lower here than Kathmandu and Dhulikhel, it is hot and close.

We drive down a narrow road dotted with shacks. Children stand and stare. There are black puddles of oily water and mangy dogs. A dust haze turns the evening light a sickly yellow. We turn into the hotel entrance. These are the grounds of the 'old-style Tibetan hotel'. How these words strike a chill in my heart, despite the Tibetan connection, I have heard too much travel agent's jargon. Yet there are flowerbeds and a lawn; the hotel yellow ochre with a balcony at the front.

As we climb down stiffly from the bus, a light plane takes off from the airport with a tremendous roar, throwing up great eddies of dust. As it springs off the tiny runway, it appears to be on course to run straight into that same precipitous mountainside we just came down in the bus. At the last moment, it banks steeply and executes a tight turn, while still only a hundred feet in the air.

Suddenly going back on that awful road doesn't seem such a bad option after all.

13

We stand about in the dusty lobby with its dead plants. It is decorated with fly-spotted pictures of faded mountains joined up (badly) in sequence. I go outside and sit in the garden. It's cooler here. I look round, searching for joined-up mountains, but the sky is blank. A dusty light glows orange as the sun goes down. I can see the foothills climbing darkly away from the town, but there are no great mountains, anywhere. Still, if the pictures in the lobby are to be believed, they must be close.

At last we are given our keys and we trudge up the stairs, along the marble corridor. There are Tibetans everywhere, with cross-over overalls, once white. They smile and say *Namaste*, and one shows me my room, right down the end of the first floor corridor.

The room is entirely beige. Some of this is due to old paint, an indefinable dinginess. A giant fan on the ceiling, and a grubby bathroom with a mouldy shower curtain. I am past caring. I strip off gingerly and stand in the bath under the eccentric shower for long minutes, washing away the grime of the journey. There are two very small grey towels. After I discover I have flooded the floor – the shower is leaking – I use them to mop up before the water reaches the carpet. From the look of it, this has happened before.

I unpack a bit, then switch on what I think is the light switch. This one turns out to be the fan, which starts up like a helicopter with such power that it blows my knickers all over the floor, and sends my papers into the air.

My room is overlooked by houses just over the wall. I crawl about half-naked, pulling the dusty curtains closed, before I can finish dressing. It's very hot and stuffy. Drawing back the curtains again, I wrestle with the mosquito grill till I can get cooler air into the room.

Ah! I had forgotten that smoky, spicy smell of Nepalese towns. One window looks over shanty-town huts, a garden and a courtyard. From there, a lot of noise floats up. Someone is laughing, and a baby screams. The other window looks over the valley. The sun is poised to set in a smoky orange ball, beyond those insubstantial, misty hills.

I do like sunsets in Nepal. They feel romantic and dreamy. One doesn't notice the other things so much, and there always seem to be a pipe player ready on cue to start up his wandering tune. But this lone musician is immediately drowned out by loud pop music from an Indian radio station. I hope that won't go on all night....

The Tibetans stand in the doorway of the dining room, smiling. They have obviously gone to a great deal of trouble with an approximation of Western food. But there is a general air of gloom in the group as we wrestle with a glutinous, lozenge-shaped mass of rice, a dozen or so brittle chips and a broken-spirited tomato subjected to some unimaginable cooking process. Sharma actually looks ill. The plates and cups are faded pink melamine, chipped with a distant pattern of roses. Somehow the pinkness makes it worse.

The littlest Tibetan, who appears to be the cook, beams wider than the rest, full of pride. He wears a red baseball cap at a jaunty angle which fits well with his round, wrinkly, ageless face, and his plastic baseball jacket. The assistant cooks stand behind him with their cross-over aprons, nodding their approval as we wrestle with the congealed remains, smiling our thanks.

The walls of the dining room are painted with a frieze – pictures of Tibet. All they have lost; yaks with high-heeled hooves springing over stylised blue hills, frozen clouds and emerald grass, a river flowing in the valley. But no people. Perhaps the artist wasn't very good at people. He certainly wasn't very good at yaks. But maybe, after all, these Tibetan exiles see their land as empty now.

Exiles – a powerful word. No Dalai Lama in the Potala, monasteries destroyed. Too much lost. Too many mistakes. *'Mistakes were made'* – the Chinese Government's own words – during the Cultural Revolution. But then, that is in the past. Attempts are being made to rebuild the surface, to put the monks back, so tourists can come and stare and, going away, feel they have seen the 'real Tibet'.

I am reading Catriona Bass: *Inside the Treasure House*. She describes how the monastery she visited in a remote region of Tibet had been destroyed, but in such a way that it looked as though it had all happened centuries before. During the fuel shortages of the Cultural Revolution, 'work-units' were sent out to scavenge for fuel. A Tibetan woman describes how the workers stripped the roof and wall timbers from the fabric of the monasteries, how lorries came back loaded with altars and bits of broken Buddhas. The carved covers of the sacred books were taken out of the rubble to be used as wash boards. Broken altar ends were saved for children's slates; drums and cymbals, which once provided the music for the sacred ceremonies, were used in parades to honour Chairman Mao. Then wind, sun and frost finished the task the Cultural Revolution had begun. All that was left was a ruin, looking as though it had taken centuries to decay.

The Buddha himself would have understood the impermanence of all such material things, their recycling into other forms. An irony there. However, it is in the teaching, the deeper religious life, so tied up with the Tibetan sense of identity, that an incalculable heritage is being lost, the lifeblood seeping away; a nation's cultural soul. The Chinese are rebuilding monasteries, but the teaching may be forbidden. Outward religious forms are allowed, the deepest teaching often not. So the Wisdom leaves, and only a shell remains. An empty land. Our hosts still smile for us, despite the fact that until recently we in Britain would not even officially receive the Dalai Lama for fear of offending the Chinese (that was in the 90's but not that much has changed in 2009).

Plots are afoot. Glen and I have hatched a conspiracy to produce a birthday cake for Sue. At the end of the meal it is borne in by one of the cooks, a huge edifice of cream, crowned by grubby candles. Sue is overcome, perhaps as much by the thought of having to eat some of this concoction, but she puts on a brave face. We hadn't meant it as a penance. She blows out the candles and we all sing *Happy Birthday* and clap, including the Tibetans.

I sleep really deeply, not even remembering until the middle of the night that I have neglected my ritual of barricading the door. I am too tired to care, and oddly, in this dingy little room in this dingy hotel, I feel safe. Maybe this is something in my mind. Anyway, I go back to sleep, only woken again at dawn by the sound of someone tapping on my window. I spring out of bed, as much as one can spring while entangled in a down sleeping bag, and peer out fearfully. A mynah bird stares back at me with unwinking eyes. It hops along the windowsill, tap, tap, tapping again with a sharp sound on the wooden frame of the mosquito mesh. Perhaps the mesh is full of insects. Anyway, he seems to want to stay, and is not afraid.

I part the curtains on the other windows. Early morning, the sun just up. There, filling the whole sky, is an enormous mountain, glimmering like a ghost of itself through the morning mist. It hadn't been there when I went to sleep. Now it is rearing above me, touched by rosy light.

Without even bothering to get dressed, I rush out of my room, down the still-sleeping corridor, up the second flight of stairs and through an open door onto the flat roof.

I am alone in the morning. The mountains, hidden from us yesterday behind a blank sky, are all there. Those same joined-up mountains of the fly-spotted picture, still phantoms in the haze, but indisputably there, at last. Even as ghosts, their power is breathtaking. They hang above me, filling the largest part of the world. Machhapuchhare, Fishtail, the Holy Mountain, which filled my window when I woke, is a jagged sword cleaving the sky, standing in front of the whole Annapurna range.

They do not show their faces fully yet, these great mountains I have come so far to see, only their misty forms. I cannot yet see glaciers, nor crevasses nor arêtes, and before the day is out they may fade again, leaving only a memory, a blank sky. But now, alone at dawn, I have all this to myself.

The town still sleeps. Looking out from this concrete roof, beyond the Tibetan house on the corner, the gardens and the poinsettia trees, the whole sky is mine. These mountains have the power to make me weep with joy. I share this moment with no one.

14

We are travelling through the suburbs of this Wild West shanty town with its rickshaws, bicycles, buses, taxis, and scruffy dogs. Puddles shine in the early morning. Men stand about smoking and talking.

I look beyond the scattered houses, their vegetable plots, goats and beehive-shaped haystacks. The mountains are still there, but, as the sun mounts in the sky, they grow fainter still, as though they were only dreams after all.

We are more cheerful after a good breakfast. No more Western imitations. Did someone complain? It wasn't me. Now we have omelettes, black aromatic tea, fresh baked bread in woven baskets, thick, glutinous porridge with hot milk and jam.

Some of the group are still suffering from stomach upsets. I have recovered, but Adrian, who had been taking antibiotics since the beginning, looks really bad. He has to leave when the porridge arrives. Whey-faced, he says gloomily, 'Both ends,' when I ask him how he is. One of the girls is really sick and Sharma looks wan. It may have been the Western food last night. Yet he still smiles that all-encompassing warm smile, like the sun coming out.

I am rather nervous at this test, my first really long day on the trail. Most of the others are already 'blooded' by that hot day on the ridge, the day Sharma and I went to see the sadhu. Was that only two days ago? Worlds of experience have passed since then. Every day changes us.

The bus drops us at the road end, the beginning of a trail. We are walking up to Sarangkot, and we wander for a mile along a flat track, in dappled shadow. Just as I begin to think how pleasant it all is, how undemanding, the trail steepens to orange sand and slabs of rock. The sun clamps down. I begin to feel the heat.

I have two bottles of water with me, but the seals look a bit suspect. We had been warned before we came that empty bottles are being refilled and resold. Not too tricky here perhaps, but higher up in the villages they are sometimes refilled in the local ditch. One of the seals on my bottle is definitely broken. I decide to put a *Potable Aqua* tablet in it.

We stop by a shack by the side of the trail, a village weaving centre. We go inside. It's very dark, and hard to see the looms, but when we get used to the dimness, we see women are working at handlooms in a low shed. The looms clack. A young girl smiles at me. They have goods to sell hanging from the roof, in traditional colours, faded red, green and white;. little purses with strings woven out of the cloth. I buy two for the girls. There are also red, green and white *topi* – the Nepalese caps.

At the far end of the shed, wonderful cloths are laid out, thick like carpets: earth colours, fresh greens, cream the colour of meadow-sweet, the sandy red of clay banks, designs of leaves and flowers, and a lovely cloth with deep green leaves woven into it, which I buy.

Sharma and I walk together, talking books. He wants to know all about publishing. He tells me a friend of his is the editor of a Nepalese magazine. He would like to send him the poem I wrote at Dhulikhel. Would I mind? (*It is later published in Nepal Vision and then in The Kathmandu Post*).

Not for the first time, I think to myself that the whole country is like a poem, and we are walking through it. Sharma tells me about Nepalese poets. We have a long conversation despite the fact I am gasping like a stranded fish in the heat, stopping to gulp down water, taking pictures and using my tape recorder. He says he doesn't mind my recording him, although last year an American woman kept asking him about politics, sticking a tape recorder under his nose, which was embarrassing.

Two girls are squatting by the side of the trail, one of them standing in a hole grubbed out of the bank, the other squatting over a sack heaped with red earth. The group seems to have walked past without noticing, but we stop and greet them – '*Namaste!*' Sharma explains they are digging out the earth from the trailside to paint their houses. The girls grin and show us the red clay. They are only little, about eight or nine. Shortly afterwards we pass some of the houses, where the red wash has been used, rich orange red, the windows painted a brilliant blue. There are striped pink and white mattresses hanging on a beam to air in the sun. A little black pig lies in the dust, snoring. Three men in bright sweaters and shirts are playing the Nepalese version of shove ha'penny on a terrace overlooking the valley. A chicken, the colour of the walls, sits broodily in an abandoned *doko*. Two pale chocolate, newborn goats are curled up together, their hooves on each other's backs.

In a patch of sharp sun and shadow, an old woman is bending down to a tiny boy. He raises his hands to her, in an ageless gesture of trust and supplication. She gives him something and he runs away. There is a notice on the tin-roofed house beside her: COLD DRINKS LEMU COCA COLA. The continuous stream of the past runs through us. Yet here, in the sign on a tin-roofed house, is also the beginning of the future.

The village looks prosperous. We stop for a few moments and buy bottles of Coca-Cola, standing about in the sun, watching the life. Children come and beg for rupees. Reluctantly, we refuse. It's hard, but we are mindful of Annabel's dictats. It is enough to be here, for the moment.

I don't think I am going to make the last part to the top. Only Sharma, walking beside me, urging me upwards, helps me to struggle on. It's so hot and I am very dehydrated. This is a busy trail, the only day when we will walk in a proper trekking area, the first part of the increasingly popular Annapurna Circuit. It shows. The differences are obvious already. There is some litter and the children beg. On the back trails around Dhulikhel, which led nowhere and were not much frequented by trekkers, the children had not learned to beg, merely asking us for our time, occasionally a pen or a sweet, but mostly nothing. There was no litter there. From tomorrow we will again be on those village trails, away from the popular circuits.

Meantime, above me, there is a great hill, and I have to get up it, my breath coming in gasps. I have to stop every few yards to lean against the wall. The air is so hot I can hardly take it in. I am full of apologies, but Sharma only laughs and says *'Just a few more yards to the golden apple!'* (the story we had been telling each other earlier). It makes me smile and try harder. I stagger on. Finally, much behind the rest, I get to the top. Would I like to go on further, a last half mile up a very steep track to a fort, a *kot* on the summit? No! I don't want to take another step. Sharma and I elect to wait at the tea stop for the others to return. I am selfishly encouraged to see that most of the group are sweating and out of breath. Perhaps if I didn't stop so often to take pictures, I wouldn't get so far behind.

This is a sophisticated tea stop, in a village with one or two shops selling bottled water and Coca Cola. There is even a little café. I buy bottled Coke at an open-fronted stall, and joy of joys, a big bar of Cadbury's Milk Chocolate. We sit for a while on the terrace outside the café. The warm wind comes flowing up to us from the valley, stroking with soft fingers. I can look down towards the sacred lake, thousands of feet below. We can't see the big mountains now, but there are folds of distant foothills, the pale shining shape of the lake beneath.

A woman in a big hat is sitting on one of the chairs surveying the scene. She seems to have been transported from outer space and dropped here by helicopter. In a long, flowing red dress and huge straw hat, she sits facing the wind. Her dress blows gracefully behind her as she looks out across the hills and the distant lake, her face set in ecstasy, like a heroine from a Henry James novel. She is telling the whole world – in American – that she is staying in *'the most impossibly elegant hotel you could imagine'*, on the edge of Phewa Tal, the sacred lake. The hotel is called Fishtail Lodge. *'Could you ever find anything more perfect?'* How has she got up here in the first place? It's a mystery.

I wander about the village where a few stalls are laid out. One is selling jewellery. I smile at the old man and pick up a lovely green necklace. Is it jade? He says yes, but it can't be. Still it's pretty. I have brought no jewellery with me. It is only R.250. Naively, I don't like to bargain, though I know I should. I'll buy it anyway....

We set off down the trail again, in a different direction. It is definitely more prosperous here than above Dhulikhel. The houses are lovely, two-storey, tin roofs in very good condition – Gurung houses with those red walls and carved, blue-painted windows.

The trail itself is excellent. Hundreds and hundreds of deep stone steps, carved out heaven knows how long ago. Going down and down, I get the leg shakes. We walk down for more than three hours. There are white blossoms here, beside the trail and the silk cotton tree splashes brilliant red across the deep green undergrowth. We see the first breathtaking scarlet rhodo-dendrons.

I lose track of time. My hips ache. Here the trail is so narrow we have to go in single file, one step, one step, one step. It is quite humid under the jungly trees, but I am glad of the shade. I walk with Clive who, meaning well, instructs me on the finer points of photography.

At last, the trail flattens out and we are in a village again. There is a tea shack beside the path. An old woman squats by a hearth in the entrance to her hut, where a fire burns under a huge blackened cauldron.

There are plastic beakers beside the hearth, black with crawling flies. Sharma sits cross-legged on the floor, smiling beatifically on the world, unperturbed by anything. He takes the beaker the old woman hands to him, speaking to her in some dialect; any one of a number he speaks fluently. We have been told it is OK to drink out of the glasses as long as we tip a little of the boiling liquid from the side to sterilise the cup. The old woman too smiles at us all, whether we have bought her tea or not.

I sit on the wall, with the smoke of the fire going up, the whisper and crackle of it, the flames pale in the fierce sun, strong in the shadow, the old woman squatting beside her pot. Sharma sits like a yogi on the earth floor, withdrawn now into himself, as he does. We are all entirely at peace with one another. The moment *is*. That's all I can say.

Continuing down the path, we come to the rice fields beside the lake, dry now. There are low clay walls round each field for when the rains do come. Irrigation! I learnt about that in Geography a long time ago, on fly-buzzing, boring afternoons – black and white pictures to colour in, women in saris bending over rice fields. As insignificant in my world as those tedious photocopied maps of the Yorkshire coal fields, which seemed then, from my home in East Anglia, just as far away.

Now. Colour in a paddy field. Colour in a brilliant sari. Black cattle. Red earth. A brilliant green lake shimmering in the distance. I was never any good at Geography, but now I am walking in a picture which has jumped off the page, and I am part of it all.

A boy comes up alongside me. He looks about ten, but then they mostly do. We talk about school and England, his house and the weather. His English is good, but he begins to irritate me with constant requests for chocolate.

'Have you chocolate? Chocolate please!'

He is very persistent. I have half a bar left from the tea shop, a bit melted, which I'm tempted to give him. Then I remember the hordes of children we have walked through this afternoon, and which we have just managed to escape. We have had to say 'No' to them all, hardening our hearts when asked for rupees, pens or sweets. If I give this boy chocolate, the bush telegraph will be in operation within minutes, and we will be plagued again.

'We have been having a good conversation. Why do you have to ask for things? I thought we were friends.'

The boy smiles, unabashed. We talk for a while. The chocolate burns a hole in my conscience. I have turned so many children down this afternoon. He asks again. It is getting harder to say 'No.'

Just when I weaken, and decide I have to give in, he looks across towards the lake and says he has to go. Without asking again for anything, he waves happily at me, turning off onto a side path which leads through the rice fields. In sudden haste, feeling bad, I scrabble about in my bumbag for the chocolate and call him back. He thanks me gravely and sprints away.

A short while later he returns. As though he were my own child, I deliver another homily.

'Surely you haven't eaten all that chocolate already! You'll be sick!'

He shakes his head, laughing up at me. 'I don't eat it!'

He stops, takes hold of my arm and points towards the sacred lake.

'You see that woman, See, see! Down there in the red sari. That is my mother.'

Framed against the sacred lake, a few hundred yards away, a group of women in saris are picking stones from the fields, *dokos* on their backs.

'Yesterday my sister died. Now my mother must carry all the stones from the field by herself! She is very, very tired. The chocolate was for her, to make her strong. Thank you. Now she is very happy!'

I remember our bus journey the day before, how we stopped on the mountain road because a child had been killed. How we had passed by her, the little girl with black hair lying in the dust. I think of that other woman squatting by the cruel tarmac, her face shrouded in her sari, the others running down the road, their faces marked by that same grave look I see on the boy's face now, as he talks about his sister dying, only yesterday. Could it have been the same family? Surely it is too far away? One way or another, the tragedy of death is very close....

Before I can say anything more, to make any reparation, he vanishes, not back towards the river, but away above me on an upper path. Is he going home? Why had he come running back to me? He hadn't asked for anything more. Was it just to say thankyou? I'll never know.

I walk on down the path, alone, between the dry rice fields, my eyes blurred with tears. For all of us. For the gap between our worlds. For my own foolish self, who so presumed.

15

This evening the restaurant has been invaded by a party of South Koreans, who overwhelm us, pushing and shoving, swooping round the corridors in synchronicity. They settle at a long table in the dining room, a chattering flock of starlings. Once in a while during the meal someone stands up, says a few words and is enthusiastically applauded by everyone, including himself. Probably in their honour, we are eating Chinese/Korean-style food this evening.

Halfway through the meal, the lights go out, clearly a common occurrence. Within minutes, candles are placed on our tables. When we leave the dining room, there are candles on every step of the shabby marble staircase. Now, by candlelight, the floor blooms with its own inner shine, rose-coloured, reflecting the light, a rather plain spinster transformed by romance. The down-at-heel hotel becomes something other than itself – an outpost on the frontier, its austerity dressed by candle-light and shadows, smiling Tibetan faces glowing beyond the candles.

I climb up onto the roof once more, and look out over the dark town, then northwards towards those mysterious, glimmering mountains. The moon has not yet risen, but overblown cabbage roses of stars tremble as though they would fall out of the sky, casting their own light on the snow slopes.

One or two of us have spent the evening arguing about how many atoms there are in the Universe. Strange that so much around us makes us think in this metaphysical way, as I did at Pashupatinath – Brahma, the 'being' of the Universe, the Creator, and Shiva, Destroyer/Creator, mirrored in those *chaityas* on the river bank; counting the atoms in the Universe, Creation and Destruction in the same gods; black holes and quarks; the transient nature of being; atomic theory anticipated over and over in an ancient stone shrine. Are we only now finding out what other cultures have known for so long?

Hearing the phone ring in the deserted lobby, I rush downstairs in time to see the sleepy receptionist emerge from a back room. And it's for me! A miracle. It must be about five pm in England. How far away it all seems, not just in terms of miles.

Will I ever have the words? I cannot begin to tell them the real things. How I am changed. I have been in another place. Despite all that loving and missing, caring and worrying, I am utterly content. Duty-bound, conscientious, fussing about them all, yet for the first time in my life I feel truly alive. It's a paradox I can't explain.

At four thirty I am woken by what sounds like roller-skating on the roof. I struggle into half-clothes (the track suit I have slept in plus trainers) and hurry up the stairs. Machhapuchhare gleams, misty in the pre-dawn sky. But instead of yesterday's shining solitude, thirty South Koreans are doing their morning exercises. They don't even greet me, just crash about in unison doing Tai Chi.

When they finish, they storm over to the balcony where I am standing, pushing me out of the way, as though I don't exist, to pose for group photographs.

Retreating to the far end of the balcony, where the view is not nearly so good, I stand on my own, watching the gentle light, gold and rose on distant snows. Others come up to join me. Sharma and Annabel and unfortunately (how unkind I am) Clive, with his six cameras, all with his name printed in woven capitals down the side of the strap.

Annabel takes charge at breakfast and orders curd for Sue's friend who is still sick. It's been too many days. Curd, she says, destroys the bad bugs in the stomach. I have heard this before and make a mental resolve to take it from the beginning, if I *ever* come here again. *If.* Adrian has recovered and intends to walk with us today. Thin before, now he is emaciated. He hasn't had a happy time in Nepal.

We drive across a bridge where a low river winds between sandy banks, before slipping through a narrow gorge. It's so far down, the river is only a glinting metallic thread somewhere in the dark. During the monsoon, it would be a different story. As we drive further down the mountainside, we can look down at the river, where it flattens out. Buses and coaches have been driven down to be washed, and men are crawling over them with long-handled brooms, shouting and singing as they scrub roofs and windows.

On the far side of the bridge, crowds of people are wandering about in a wooded area. Young birch trees flutter their leaves like golden pennies. A bus passes us with schoolchildren, dark skins glowing against white shirts. The pupils lean out of the window and shout 'GOOD MORNING, SIR!' We wave back. I think how jolly it all is.

Then Glen spots a large shape hanging from a tree. We all crane out of our seats to look. The bus stops in a jam. We are caught, voyeurs on the road, as before when the child had been killed. In the centre of a copse, the dark slim body of a young man, dressed in white shirt and dark trousers, is turning slowly among the Spring birch trees. It is the time of the Festival, of rejoicing, but perhaps, for him, it was too much to bear.

We move on at last. In the midst of death, we are in life. Since I came here, to Nepal, that has become clearer to me.

Rupa Tal. Another sacred lake. I am used to being on the water, but these boats look really unsafe, unstable with no draught at all. Water is seeping in already. And three of us will get in to each boat with the boatman. At least we will be going out in formation, so if one of us sinks...

The lake is a bit like Windermere, and about the same size. I get in gingerly. The boat rocks violently, despite my seaman's technique drummed in by years of climbing into a pram dinghy in a Force 6.

It's a long way. The boatman sits in the stern, wielding a single paddle. We don't go very fast. We creep past tawny brown, dusty hills, and dark green patches of glassy water where trees shadow the lake. White egrets perch, silent and watchful, on the dead branches, not even bothering to fly away as we pass. More flat-bottomed boats glide alongside, going the other way. The men smile and say *Namaste* and we contrive to say *Namaste* with as much dignity as we can muster, without tipping the boat. In places there are little waves. The water is clear.

At last we come in sight of the shore at the far end of the lake, and we land on mudflats. Someone holds the bow while I clamber out inelegantly, a tangle of cameras and Leki stick, as always. We cross the muddy, dried-up floor, which must be covered by water in the monsoon. On the far side is thick woodland, almost a forest, and a narrow sandy track winding upwards. An old man waits for us in the shade of the trees. He speaks to our local guide for a few minutes, and word comes back that he is warning us that a few weeks before, someone was killed by a tiger on this path.

My nerves are a bit on edge after this. I thought tigers only lived in the Terai. How a thicket of trees subtly changes whether or not there might be a tiger in there!

This nervousness is made worse when, getting a bit behind, I hear a terrific yelling ahead of us, and much crashing about in the undergrowth. A youth jumps out of the bushes and runs towards me, shouting and waving a curved knife like a cutlass. I stand aside as others jump down out of the trees, and run towards me, they too brandishing fiendish-looking kukris, like a raiding party in a pirate film. There isn't much I can do but just stand still on the narrow track. But, blessed relief, they run straight past me, away through the trees and down towards the lake. Sharma comes back to see if I'm OK. He explains that the men were hunting a rabbit! (I thought it would be the tiger at least)...

I struggle up what has been described by Annabel as a 'gentle incline' (for the encouragement of invalids). It's staggeringly hot, hotter than on any other day. Must be close to 100 F, with very little shade and no breeze. The path gets steeper. I am through my first bottle of water. Too hot to speak, I trudge on in my own hellish little world, dying for shade and cool.

At last we stop by a platform - a *chautaara* - under a pipal tree, to wait for the others. They have elected to walk along the lake shore rather than take the boat.

Here the pipal tree spreads its branches and its blessed shade over the *chautaara*. A whole family lives here in a thatched hut with their animals. Below, there are a few tiny terraced fields. There are at least three girls of various sizes, one with long straggly bunches in her hair tied up with string, a mother and a baby. I suppose the father is out, maybe with his sons. Annabel tells us that the previous two parties stopped here in November, when the baby had just been born.

The tree and hut seem to run into one another. They must share everything. The family's water nourishes the tree, and in return it gives them shade. The animal shelter, where a water buffalo and a calf browse away the hot hours, is thatched with dead leaves from the tree. A tin kettle stands among the roots beside a battered tin bowl. The pipal tree is sacred. There is always one planted at porters' stopping places and in the centre of a village, usually beside a banyan tree.

Looking into the interior of the hut, I can see there is only the earth floor, a few mats and a roll of cotton bedding. At least six people live in this small space, yet there is an atmosphere of happiness and peace. I think of my family, all five of us, jammed into the caravan in the rain, fighting and whingeing, and I'm ashamed. On this platform, in the shade of the pipal tree, is everything in the world; a few minute terraced fields, carved out of the slope, glowing green now with new barley, a thatched shelter for the animals, a kettle and a bowl. Bedding. Shelter. Shade.

We stand awkwardly under the great tree, whose roots spread out around the hut. The lady of the house stands in the open door, her girl children touching her skirts. She recognises Annabel and Sharma and smiles delightedly. The girl with the bunches is wearing a miniature version of her mother's outfit, a pale pink tie-string blouse (*cholo*), a *patuka* (waist cloth) made of off-white rags, and a short blue *lunghi*, a kind of Nepalese sarong. She grins gappily at us, proudly picking up the baby for us to see. He is chubby and healthy. She lifts him high into the air, and everyone laughs. Then she lays him on the mat, where he kicks, gurgling happily.

Family planning has not made much impact in the hill villages, where infant/child mortality is one of the highest in Asia. In places like the Kathmandu valley where land is scarce and pollution problems worsen by the year, population growth is a real problem. The last figures I saw put the growth at 2.6 per cent a year, compared with 1 per cent in the UK. But here, a healthy baby is still seen as a blessing. It is hard to change attitudes, especially when more than twelve babies in a hundred will die before they reach one year old and more than 25 per cent will not survive childhood.

I look down, past the tiny glowing fields, the neat thatch on the animal hut, towards the distant blue of the lake. The family have everything here. They aren't starving. But if one year the rains fail, with the impact of global warming, or floods carry away the fields, or if the father falls ill, it could be a different story. I hope it never happens, that this little family goes on living here beside the trail as long as the tree lasts, in perfect balance.

The others come struggling up the path. We sit about while they get their breath, and then we climb on in the heat. This is not at all like the previous day on the beginning of the Annapurna circuit. Children come and walk beside us on their way to school, in their Western-style uniform, showing us their books. Others just touch us and hold our hands. But no one begs. It's hard to communicate, but they smile. That's enough.

Further on, we pass a school entrance. The headmaster comes out and speaks to Sharma. They are asking for money for materials, as they have run out completely. We collect some rupees, and the headmaster insists on giving us a receipt. This seems a very good alternative to giving in to begging.

Clive and I go into the playground. Children gather round in the dust, smiling and touching. Some wear headscarves like Muslim children. The young teacher in a red T-shirt and jeans starts the children singing a song about Nepal. We record them on our tape recorders and play it back to them. Once again I feel that embarrassment about flashing around twentieth century hardware. They shriek with laughter and we all have a good time.

Above the stone lintel is the mysterious message *THIS SCHOOL WAS FOUNDED IN THE YEAR 2023*. Sharma explains that in Nepal there is a different system of counting years. It looks odd, as though we have walked into the future. In one way, here at this school, I suppose we have. These children, the first generation to be educated, *are* the future. Nothing will ever be the same again.

At one o'clock we finally stop for lunch in a village square, which is also a porters' stopping place. There are those piles of stones by the tree again, built up into a *chautaara*, where the porters can take the weight off their packs by resting their loads. Ancient pipal and banyans have bound their roots into the side of the trail, and an iron water pipe trickles water onto a stone slab. Somewhere a bulbul bird echoes the watery sound in the quiet. We can look down and down over green forests towards the distant lake. Have we really climbed this high?

The village has some rudimentary electricity, if the poles and wires are to be believed. We have passed men on the trail with girders and poles on their backs. Sharma explains that these are part of a hydro-electric project. The steel poles are so long the porters have to walk crabwise up the trail. Charlie Nye-Smith makes the point in his book, *Travels in Nepal*, that electricity may not be the blessing it is always supposed to be, in helping to prevent deforestation. With electric light, the family stays up later and burns more fuel. But Sharma tells us that as the fumes from kerosene stoves are contributing a lot to chest problems, electricity for cooking may help. There are no chimneys in most of the huts, so when it's cold, or in the monsoon, the door is kept shut and there is nowhere for smoke to go. But then who will be able to afford an electric stove? Nothing is quite what it seems when one starts messing about with an ancient, stable way of life, even when one is determined to do *good*! Dreadful Word.

Clean water can't have a downside, can it? The children run in and out of a thin trickle of water, cupping their hands to the pipe. Village women come with aluminium pots and fill them, leaning on the side of the concrete. They smile at us, happy to wait and watch. In all our long walk this morning, I have neither seen nor heard a stream since we left the lake. There must be water in these hills, but, in the dry season, how far must the women walk before finding water?

There is a wonderful description in Joy Stephen's book about living among the Magars, *Window Onto Annapurna*, when the water is at last laid on to the village. What a day! Remembering Joy Stephen's descriptions of the Magar women, I wonder if this may indeed be a Magar Village. There are so many different hill tribes (though most around here seem to be Gurungs), but the women's dress is right. One of them, second in the queue, is wearing a wine-coloured velvet jacket, a string of deep blue marriage beads, a lime green patuka wrapped round her waist and a pink lunghi, her hair covered in a bright green scarf. She has a beautiful, ageless face, and is so elegant that she would not disgrace a Paris catwalk (although it is an insult to think of her in such a way). She is standing by me now, smiling while she waits for her turn to fill her pot. Her little boy is up to mischief by the pump, running in and out of the water, screaming. She tells him off roundly, rubbing her back while she leans on the wall. Our eyes meet. For a moment, there is a rapport between us. I too have stood waiting in line, my back aching, while my children misbehave. It may have been in the endless queue in Safeway's, trying to keep two toddlers away from the Mars bars, but that doesn't matter. Briefly, we understand each other.

She bends with supreme grace, and lifts the pot onto her shoulder, walking back up the track with the small boy jumping and singing beside her. I have to remind myself how hard their lives must be. Impossibly hard. It's easy to fantasise. Just now, at this moment, I would exchange the soulless Safeway's queues, the metal trolleys, the cold, predatory aisles of baked beans, for a few days here among the village women. I have to remind myself that I would hate it when it rains.

We make a temporary camp among the roots of the pipal tree, where there are years of dead leaves and some huge roots to sit on. Some elect to walk on a little further to another temple but the rest of us are content to stay here. There are a few thatched huts, conical instead of square, a tiny stream with watercress, a water buffalo and her fluffy, teddy bear calf munching greenery in a gully. The mother stares at us suspiciously.

On the far side of the sandy clearing, an old man emerges from the darkness of a single story rectangular hut. He drifts out with the smoke from the doorway. He is very old, with wrinkled, blackened skin and very thin legs, finished off by rubber flip-flops. He offers us tea. I see that his roof, thatched with leaves, is a different shape from the rest.

Perhaps he is the headman of the village. The villages are organised on a *panchayat* system, village councils electing their own representative, though I don't know how democratic it is in practice. He and Sharma have a long talk, as swarms of children appear out of nowhere, wanting to look through Annabel's binoculars.

It is so peaceful here, even with children shouting. We sit among the dry leaves, drinking water and munching one another's Indian biscuits, watching the life of the village. I take some pictures. The old man, seeing my camera, comes across and asks if he can look through it. It seems that he thinks the camera *is* a pair of binoculars. Looking through the viewfinder he is disappointed to see that things look smaller, not bigger. He tries to remedy this by turning the camera upside down, then holding it further away. He doesn't have any English and I don't have any Nepali, or whatever hill dialect it is here, so it is quite hard to explain the difference between the camera and a pair of binoculars. I would probably feel much the same confusion when faced with a wooden rice thresher or an ox plough.

He obviously feels let down by the inadequacy of my equipment. I point to Annabel, who is still sitting beside the pump, patiently sharing her binoculars with fifteen assorted children. He ambles over, hoping for better things.

Sharma comes to sit behind me, with his back against the tree. I ask him about the lake. Is it sacred?

'Not very,' he says. 'Not as sacred as Phewa Lake.'

'A bit sacred? On a scale of one to ten, how sacred?'

He laughs at the thought, not offended.

'All lakes are a bit sacred. But Phewa is the most sacred of all. Yes.'

He has a way of saying 'Yes' very quietly, just by itself, and smiling that slow smile. 'Water is such a precious thing.'

Someone has seen a Red-Vented Bulbul. All lunchtime its hiccoughing song, like an interrupted waterspout, has filled the spaces in our talk. Annabel lends me her binoculars. We walk to the edge of the village, peering through the eyepiece at the trees. Eventually, I see a bright bird on a branch. I rush back to tell Sharma, who hasn't bothered to get up. He confesses he can hardly tell one bird from another, apart from sunbirds. Armed with this ammunition, I am able to show him up several times during the afternoon by asking him which birds are which. Each time he gets the giggles.

We go back to sitting under the tree for a while. I switch on my tape recorder to catch the sounds of the village and leave it on, forgetting about it for a while. I can later catch the sound fabric of the afternoon, a painting in sound, like a scent of coffee, lavender in old linen or bacon frying, only these are evocations in sound not scent, which have never before stirred me in such a way – that bulbul bird, the laughter of children, a discussion about education between Sharma and myself, the old man talking to La'al (our local guide) on the far side of the tree, the rustle of dry leaves, three people walking past us on the trail, two women with *dokos,* a man in traditional Nepalese dress, a topi and a black waistcoat with a *lunghi* below. I notice *he* isn't carrying anything. We all greet each other, *Namaste.*

At one point, when I pick up the tape recorder, but forget to switch it off, there is the sound of the zipper on my bumbag as I put it away, elephantine crashing of boots on the trail, ribald remarks, and the noise of rushing water when I catch the sound of my squatting hurriedly behind a bush, in mortal terror of being sprung by six children who have been trying to follow me in order to practise their English. I seem to have forgotten about the tiger!

16

We seem to be poised forever in some shining void, as the lake shimmers around us, a mercurial blob absorbing and reflecting light, changing shape as it runs between crumpled hills.

It hurts to look. Even with sunglasses, the light is almost too much to bear. I've built myself a shelter with my yashmak and Leki stick. I look downwards at the boards at the bottom of the boat, where water, seeping in steadily through the leaking seams, swills about my boots.

So here we are, just two boats going back. I should have walked back the last mile or so like most of the others, but laziness overcame caution and it was so hot coming down the trail. Sharma is sitting behind me, with Adrian, who is feeling a bit weak. We hang together on the water, seemingly going nowhere, despite the efforts of the boatman. A breeze springs up. Too hot to cool us down, it blows in our faces like an Aga door opening, slowing the boat even more. We have hung opposite this same lot of trees for a quarter of an hour. Adrian must weigh a lot. He's so tall. OK. I weigh quite a lot. And then there's Sharma, who is fairly well-built. No wonder the boatman, used to ferrying around short slim Nepalese, is having such a hard time.

We are floating, motionless on this burning lake like dead leaves. The same bit of shoreline, the same egrets looking down, not bothering to move. Fish flick in the watery depths. How cool it must be down there. A fishing boat glides past, going the other way, blown by the same wind which now fixes us helplessly. I am wearing factor 30 on my arms. Still I feel my skin burning. To look forwards into that intense, brutal light is like a dagger in the eyes.

I feel sorry for the boatman. No one speaks and we can hear his breathing. Hard work for a few rupees. I lean over carefully so as not to upset the boat ('Ship the boat!' speaks my phantom

father) watching the water flowing past, laughing to itself. The
water moves but we don't. If you didn't look at the shoreline and
the statues of egrets – who could move if they wanted to, unlike
us – one would have the illusion of movement, quite fast through
the water. But it *is* an illusion. Suspended here, pinned by the
relentless sun, with the wind against us, the water mocks us.

Sharma leans forward.

'Moving water. Stagnant boat,' he says softly.

A bubble of laughter wells up in me. As though he has broken
the spell, the wind drops and we begin to move forward. We
round the point which has hung tantalisingly in front of us for so
long. Just in time, as the water in the bottom of the boat is now
over the welt of my boots.

Freed from terrors, I begin to free-fall. Images float through
my mind in a way that hasn't happened for so long. There has
never been time for all this thinking. I have always been
worrying about something, not just because I am a natural
worrier (though never used to be). Simply, in the last few years,
there has always been something real to worry about. Sitting
here, in this boat, I can see it clearly, an endless procession of
worries parading past me like ghosts in chains. Not only chained
to one another, they have also been chained to me. Just when I
have laid one to rest, another gives its chain a tug and I am off
again.

But now, for a few precious moments, because Sharma has
made me laugh, I am free. I no longer think we are going to sink.
I know we will get to the shore. As on the roof when I stood
looking at Machhapuchhare in the dawn sky, I feel the joy which
once was there in me, which Life, as lived perhaps by most of us,
had leached away. For so many people like me, it must be the
same, ground down by our worries (mostly little, though not
always), caught up in the habit of worry like flies in a web.

I see in my mind the Magar woman rubbing her back while
she calls to her son. Maybe it's the same for us all. Yet she looked

so serene, so peaceful, so accepting. Is that good or bad?

As the boat glides towards the far shore, I think about the days we have passed through. How I am changed. How narrow my life has been till now. Stagnant even. Moving water. Stagnant boat. Life has flowed past me. Occasionally I have put my hand over the side, and guddled about in the water, fearful of what I might find, feeling the pressure of the moving water like jelly on my hands. The waters have moved round me and I have hung there in my own leaky coracle, my own little microcosm, worries, preconceptions and all.

The boat hisses through the mud at the lake edge as we come to the end of the lake. Sharma helps me out. My legs are stiff from sitting for so long, my arms bright red. The others are waiting on the jetty. We have been on the lake a long time. I am glad to be on dry land, but reflective. I don't want to talk much on the way back, hugging that sense of being on the edge of something, on a precipice looking down. An exhilarating feeling.

'Nepal is there to change you, not for you to change it'. It's on all the T-shirts.

I sleep lightly here, not exhausted despite those long hours of walking. In any case, the dogs make deep sleep impossible. I am aware of them all night long, half in dreams. It's the dog next door which starts it all, and is responsible for setting the whole lot off. I love dogs (I have four of my own) but I could cheerfully throw a large rock at the one next door, the leader of the orchestral wailing which starts exactly on 10.30 pm, just as I am thinking about sleep, but is not quite there.

First next door's dog starts the Hound of the Baskervilles routine, then the one over the road, and then, one by one, every dog in Pokhara (barring the dead ones) joins in the chorus. Last night there wasn't even a moon to start them off. And they go on all night until just before dawn. Sharma has christened them *The Owl Dogs of Pokhara*. What really gets me is the way they sprawl about all day in the middle the road, building up their strength for the next night's onslaught, giving good folk pain by looking dead. I must be soft, even worrying. They are a completely feckless lot.

However, I wake refreshed today. This in spite of the howling dogs, the mule trains passing at dawn with tinkling bells (rather nice), the late night laughter in the streets, and that tame mynah bird pecking at the window frame. Oh, yes, and then there are those kamakazi mosquitoes which have somehow evaded my loo paper barrier on the waste pipe. There can be few noises quite as unnerving as a mosquito passing one's left ear in a whining dive while one is peacefully asleep. It can't be good for my heart to sit up quite that suddenly. We take two kinds of malaria tablets (one lot every day, the other lot once a week) though Annabel says there isn't any malaria here. It is even supposed to be eradicated in the Terai. Most advice says take the tablets anyway.

I am on the roof by five but the mountains have almost faded away, ghosts of their ghosts. In the haze I can hardly see them. The air is fresh, the town waking up as the sun pops over the misty ridge. I'm glad to be here. This morning the Koreans are having a day off from Tai Chi, or perhaps they have gone elsewhere to plug into those primal energies. Anyway, I've got it to myself.

After breakfast, I wave goodbye to the others as they go off on the bus. They are going to do another long ridge walk, but just for today, I have done enough walking. I am going to sit for a while in the garden of the hotel, writing my diary, peacefully.

I have grown to love this little hotel, with its smiling Tibetan faces. So I sit among the flowers, relishing the peace, with nothing but the sound of water from the hosepipe sprinkling the garden, and the street sounds beyond the gate – an Indian radio playing pop, someone shouting, the screech of brakes as yet another cyclist tries to commit suicide under the wheels of a taxi.

I find myself more alone these days, thinking my thoughts, feeling everything around me. What happened to that woman who made everyone laugh? Inside me now is a stillness that was never there before.

Out of the corner of my eye, I see Sharma crossing the lawn. He sees I am writing, and quietly, in that tranquil manner of his, he settles himself on a table in the lotus position. I glance up, but his eyes are closed in concentration. He has offered at breakfast to take me into Pokhara to find some books which he thinks I should have. He doesn't want to walk today.

I finish writing and he comes over while I sort out my papers. I'm worried that, on his day off, he might not want to be landed with taking me about the place. After all, he gets so little free time. Even in the evenings he is always bombarded with questions, which he tries his best to answer, in his almost perfect English. I try to say this, but get in a muddle. He only laughs and says it is his choice too. We are easy now in each other's company.

A hoopoe flies onto the lawn and struts about, exotic with its flirty crest and barred wings, its dun, gold and amber plumage the colour of those dry hills. It runs right up to us. We watch it, caught up in the magic of its presence, as it probes its beak into the ground like an oyster catcher, stabbing the dry grass.

Sharma and I have a whispered argument about what it is called. It is *not* a kingfisher. But, although he may not know its name, he has seen the bird 'sometimes' in the hills, above the sacred lake. It's very rare for it to come down from the woods into the town, and he had never seen it in Pokhara.

The bird stays on the lawn. I watch it for a while, as it runs jerkily, its head bobbing among the marigolds, like a scurrying housewife picking up after her kids. Its amber plumage weaves a darker shade into the searing orange of the flowers. I feel privileged that it is close to us, sharing this empty garden.

At last, it runs once more across the lawn, its crest comes up, and with a flash of barred wings it flies off, back to its peaceful woods. It's nice to think of it up there, flitting, jay-like, among the dark trees, where no one sees it.

We walk out of the gate of the hotel and onto the road. Most people have explored Pokhara on foot, but I have only been as far as the stall over the road which sells water. We go down to the tarmac road and walk down towards the lake. Sharma is humming his song under his breath as he walks. I notice he does that sometimes. Always the same song when he seems happy.

It's very hot and huge trucks thunder past, spraying us with dust. There's no pavement, just an earth bank at the side of the road, and an open ditch. It's quite difficult to avoid the bikes, cars and lorries and still stay out of the stinking puddles. I am glad when we turn off the main road and begin to walk down towards the lake.

Sharma asks if I would like to see the Fishtail Lodge before we go to the bookshop. I have got dressed up today to do the town, in a silk top and a skirt, and although I am looking a bit wilty already, what with the dust and the heat, I reckon I could take on the Fishtail Lodge. It has lived as an exotic place in my mind ever since I heard the American woman talking about it at Sarangkot, the first day here.

It's quite a long walk to Phewa Tal, the sacred lake, down a dusty lane to a jetty area where a few people are standing about. Green water, an island on the far side. An old man is operating a raft from the island to the shore. We stand in the sun waiting for the raft to return. The lake is very clear and still, reflecting the island, which I can see is full of lowering trees.

The raft comes back, and the passengers – smart women in saris, men in traditional Nepali dress, a couple of men in Western suits – step gingerly off the tippy planks and stand, looking back at the lake. About ten of us step onto the raft, which seems rather a lot, and the raft rocks, but one of the passengers, very courteously, extends his hand to help me before Sharma can. The old man pulls on a rope which is attached to the far shore. He pulls the forward rope with a slapping rhythm which echoes, in a strangely peaceful way, over the quiet lake. As the rope behind us curves, shining droplets cascade back into the water.

We glide across the green glass. We are no more than a few minutes away from the dusty main road, the snarling traffic, the stinks of the ditch, but in the silence we are in another time. A boat shimmers along beside us. A beautiful girl in a scarlet sari is sitting in the bow with a huge bundle of leaves on her back, and a man in a matching T-shirt paddles in the stern. The green leaves, the splashes of red, the reflections in the still lake, a silver arc of diamond drops, the slapping curve of the rope, the island waiting for us on the far side, all spin together in a powerful web of magic. I am in a spell. As when we found the sadhu in the forest, I am beyond myself, simply in another place.

We reach the island. Sharma helps me off the raft, onto the path where steps wind upward into bushes and trees. We climb, one behind another, in sun and shadow. Then suddenly we burst out into full sunlight. It is a garden, but like nothing I have ever seen – colour, running water, grass, butterflies. Words from an English primer are not enough. Fountains, blue flowers, scarlet poinsettia, bougainvillea in every conceivable shade of red and yellow, a whole side of a garden house covered in orange frangipani, deep purple blossoms hanging from bushes. Emerald grass, shade and shadow, silence, except for bird song every-where and the sounds of falling water. A Garden of Eden.

All around are breathtaking butterflies, the size of two hands held in shadow play. They shimmer among the flowers. Sharma, happy with my delight, calls me here and there. 'Angela! Angela! Look at this!' I have been starved till now. My natal language is unused to this, and can only speak in clichés of this iridescent world beyond words.

I run about the gardens like a child, unselfconsciously, and Sharma laughs at my pleasure. Best of all, the huge black velvet butterflies with a shimmer of sapphires, the electric colour of the streak on the Neon Tetras fish my sister used to keep. Lighter than birds, they dance above us, leading us on. Round every corner there is another fountain, another crimson flower, more purple frangipani, more emerald grass and shining water. I want to be here for ever.

We stay and drink tea, sitting in a corner of the garden. The butterflies come to sip from the edge of the teacups, alighting in perfect balance, jewelled wings shimmering in the sun. The bookshop can wait. I sit in shade and sun, just being. After we have drunk tea, we wander again through the gardens and exploring further, skirt a barrier and walk along a forest path down to the border of the lake.

We look out over its milky sheen, to where a fishing boat hangs in silence in the exact centre. The faint shadows of Machhapuchhare and the Annapurnas float in the sky. Somewhere near here, I believe, is the King's winter palace. Does he, too, wander in gardens like these? Where shadows are on the edge of the lake, the water green and still?

We have walked so far and talked so much that now it is time for lunch. And we haven't been to the bookshop. Instead we are still, looking out at the butterflies, as we sit by the window, in this impossibly elegant place, wood and coolness, and white cloths. A bit different from our dear old hotel. Ambassadors and princes come here. You can see them in photos on the walls. Even Prince Charles was here. Glad I wore my silk top.

Sharma's friend is the manager of the restaurant, and I think a part-owner of the hotel. He treats me with great courtesy, bringing me special Nepalese vegetables to try, hot and aromatic. I am so much on a 'high' that I can't eat much. I just taste things, sharply, as though for the first time.

17

We have to get to the bookshop. This is the last chance. Tomorrow is the big walkabout, our last day. Reluctantly, we take the ferry back again, just Sharma and I and the boatman this time. Is this what is called a *char-dohar garne dungaa,* 'a coming and going boat'? Perhaps it is.

On the lakeshore, under an ancient pipal tree, a young man is playing a *saarangi* – a carved Nepalese violin. The high plaintive note falls into the silence, broken only by the slap, slap, slap, of the rope in the water.

As we glide to the far shore, the saarangi player begins to sing, a high, thin serenade, utterly Eastern, strange and sad, playing his violin with a small horsehair bow and plucking the strings, a perfect sound as we move across the still waters. I show my delight, clapping and smiling. Encouraged, he carries on singing as we come ashore, following us up the track.

Then, rather diffidently, he produces from his jacket a miniature *saarangi*, about a foot long, with wooden pegs holding the four strings, and a carved wooden body like half a giant walnut. It is all made from one piece of wood. I turn it in my hands. On the back is a carved flower. I pluck the strings. There again is that high, sad, haunting note. The very sound of this spellbound place. And yes, it plays. He produces a tiny horsehair bow, drawing it across the strings, singing softly.

I remember that, feeling a bit like the father in Beauty and the Beast, I had asked my children what they would like me to bring back for them from my travels, Harriet had said 'a musical instrument like the country' and I had been looking everywhere. I had seen the flutes in the bazaar in Kathmandu, carried around on huge 'trees' by the flute sellers. But they hadn't seemed different enough. This is perfect. But I don't know how much to pay. How can one put a price on something so lovely? It is unique, even if he has another ten saarangi hidden behind the tree (he probably does). The prayer wheel all over again. At last, with Sharma's help, we agree a price, not too much, and we walk on down the lake road. There are open-fronted shops, and lots of restaurants, a real tourist area – Europeans and Americans in hippy robes, with pony tails, sitting in the entrances to the cafes, looking intense, or spaced-out. Sharma glances at them disapprovingly. He tells me that the hippy 'problem' was really bad about ten years ago, that the Government have been trying to stamp it out. They came to smoke pot, especially here, to Pokhara, and to scrounge off the locals, who are poor enough already.

As we walk along, I catch a whiff of some dark, herby smell, which smells a bit like the 'asthma cigarettes' my grandfather used to pollute the bathroom with when he was clearing his chest. I'm pretty naïve about all this. I see a few people wandering about looking vague, and there is one Westerner lying dead or asleep outside an open-fronted shop. As with the fake dead dogs, I go past gingerly, looking to see if his chest is going up and down. Actually, it doesn't seem to be. After the glory of the Fishtail Lodge butterflies, this is a sharp reminder of the downside.

Sharma takes me into a bookstore, another open-fronted shop. The owner is very helpful. I buy Charles Nye Smith's *A Walk in Nepal*, which is very informative on the subject of Aid Projects, not always flattering. The message is that generally 'small is beautiful' and big can sometimes turn out to be a white elephant, not always addressing the needs of the country. It's all about listening to the people, and what they really need.

Sharma also wants me to get Lyda Arun's *The Art of Nepal*. We have talked so much and so long about the nature of religion in Nepal, whether it be Hinduism or Buddhism and how the two come together. Sharma says that this book explains it all very well.

Most of the books, even those not printed in Nepal, are very much cheaper here. There are lots of second-hand ones, which people sell off after trekking. We wander on down the road, laden with books, which we take it in turns to carry.

Sharma says the road runs out very soon and we will get to the lakeshore again, so we plod on in the heat, past cafes full of people. It's a raffish, colourful place. I love the lake and the gardens of the Fishtail and the mountains and all that, but Pokhara itself seems a bit seedy. It isn't the Nepalese. It's the dirty, spaced-out Westerners and a few local hangers-on who make it seem so down-at-heel. What are we doing to the world, that we come seeking peace and spiritual fulfilment, and end up despoiling?

We literally run out of road. It just stops, as though the town only crawled so far, and then gave up. The shacks and open-fronted shops peter out and there is a rough path down to the lake, shadowed by trees and *chautaara* just at the height of the bottom of the loads. Once the town runs out of people, there is just the lake, and it feels quite different. We stand looking out over the water, where there is an island in the middle and a temple half-hidden in trees. The Varahi Temple. A row of boats are tied up by the shore.

On impulse we decide to row out. Sharma finds a boatman. I tiptoe over the slippy stepping-stones at the muddy edge of the lake, wetting the hem of my skirt as I get into the boat. It is quiet and cool on the water. Flashing, dappled light from little short waves. Unfortunately, the mountains have disappeared completely behind cloud or haze. I sit watching the water, actually dabbling my hand over the side, thinking I am no longer afraid.

The temple is surrounded by ancient pipal and banyan trees, much, much older than any trees I have seen so far, with giant twisted trunks like the Ents in Lord of the Rings. They feel very holy. In fact, for the first time I get a real scary feeling of holiness which I haven't had in the same way anywhere else, not even in the sadhu's sanctuary.

Here it is *so* very old. Deep shadow and the flittering leaves of the great trees very high up, where only greenish sunlight filters through. The courtyard in front of the temple is plastered with bird droppings, and there is red powder scattered everywhere on the stone statues. There are also stains of what looks like blood. The carved doors of the temple are shut.

The only sound is a constant, soothing, cooing of doves, the only moving things, apart from the leaves stirring in the faint breeze, and us. The doves are everywhere, on every stone effigy, on the walls, flying from place to place in the grove of trees with a faint hush of wings, a flash of white high up.

We walk clockwise round the temple. As so often in Nepal, I have been instantly transported into another dimension, with a new and frightening set of feelings. Fifteen minutes ago, I was in a different place. Now I am here. How simple that sounds. But the powerful feeling of *Hereness* is indescribable. I *am* these things; the doves, the ancient trees, the blood-splashed stones, the sacred lake. It is a fairy tale, not as Walt Disney might tell it, but as our ancient memory struggled to express the power of forest and stone, the holiness of Life and Death. Once again, I don't have the words.

Halfway round, we stop and pull ourselves onto the wall, where we sit in the sun, watching the water. It is brighter here, and the shadowy holiness of the place retreats a little. Looking down, I see that there is a straight stone wall into the lake; no shore on this side of the temple, the opposite side to Pokhara. In the distance a sandy shore with a forest stretches impenetrably upwards into the foothills.

Sharma explains that this temple is one of the holiest places in Nepal, in the centre of Phewa Tal, that most sacred lake. It was a favourite place for the hippies, who came seeking spirituality. They would dive off the wall just here, where it plunges straight into the lake. Then they would swim naked to that far shore, opposite Pokhara. They would make camp on to the shore, take drugs and make 'open sexual love'. Sharma says quietly that the Nepalese people were very offended by this sacrilege. I have heard that the hippies were rounded up one night, dumped over the Indian border, where they had their names taken and told they wouldn't be allowed back.

I try to imagine the same thing happening in Westminster Cathedral. It is not as though the Nepalese people are prudish. You just have to look at the erotic carvings on the temples in Kathmandu. It is just that, to them, holy places go on being holy, even when nothing appears to be going on. They aren't just holy when rows of people in hats start singing hymns, while the rest of the time it's perfectly OK for hordes of gum-chewing tourists to trample about taking photographs. Perhaps we don't always understand that holiness is there all the time, if it is there at all.

Funny about that word 'holy'. I keep using it: a word that would hardly occur in my vocabulary (except while singing carols or hymns three times a year at Christmas, Easter and Harvest Festival). But it is the only word I have.

We jump off the wall, and carry on walking round the temple, circumnavigating the uncharted earth. Clockwise, the way the world turns in its Heaven. Doves burble peacefully above us.

I ask Sharma how he, as a Buddhist, can reconcile the animal sacrifices of the Hindu 'part' of the temple (of course it is not a case of any physical division) with his own beliefs in the sanctity of Life. He turns to me and smiles.

'Where there have been sacrifices, we release white doves.'

We climb down over the giant stones on the shore, to where the boatman is waiting. It's time to leave. A third of the way across the lake, without warning, a terrific wind springs up from nowhere, and the sunlight goes out. The same thing had happened the previous evening when we had been sitting in the garden and a violent dust storm had driven us all inside. This is more violent still. I glance down the lake. The far end, furthest away from Pokhara, has completely disappeared – just blackness, like the darkness of a winter's afternoon before snow. In a few seconds, the wind whips up short, steep waves which slap at the side of the shallow boat. There is something almost biblical about this sudden storm on the lake, adding to my fear.

I want to turn back, but Sharma, facing me, smiles reassuringly, telling me not to be afraid. He looks perfectly calm. And truthfully, it would be as hard to go back as to go on. The boatman struggles with the paddle, making no progress against the wind and waves. I am really scared. The real thing this time, not like yesterday on the lake, which seems no more than a pathetic imitation. And at least then the sun was shining.

I can hardly see the Pokhara shore, which is enveloped in mist, seeming so far away. Huge raindrops pockmark the water. Just for once, I have forgotten my waterproofs! It seemed so ridiculous a precaution on such a perfect morning. How long ago it seems.

I sit, hunched with misery and fear, wet and cold. The wind gets fiercer. Water begins to splash in a serious, intent sort of a way, over the gunwale. Where is the spirit of Empire now? I can see before me, so clearly that it might almost be there, a headline in *The Cumberland News*.

'*Local author drowns in Himalayan lake tragedy*'.

Imagination at times is a curse.

The storm breaks just above us with a terrific crash of thunder, and lightning hisses down into the lake. Are these ancient gods angry with me for walking in their sanctuary? In this sudden terrifying storm, with this black sky and these frightening waves, I am ready to believe it is so. If the boat capsized, could I swim ashore? Would anyone come to our aid? The shore where the boats are tied up is utterly deserted, swept by misty rain like an off-season beach at Blackpool. What price poetry now?

Lightning strikes the lake again, just to the side of us. There is a terrific roll of thunder. Sharma goes on smiling steadily. The waves are coming up over the side, adding to the water sloshing about in the bottom. If I ever get to shore in one piece, I will never go adventuring again. I will be good forever. Promise! I just want to go home.

How much danger are we in? It's hard to tell. Just now, home, dear wonderful home, would be the best place in the whole world. I am simply not up to this. I was a fool to come. I should stay in my own backyard, and be content.

'Don't worry. It will be OK. Really, it will be OK!'

Sharma smiles his slow, quiet, unworried smile. The wind eases off a little. Perhaps we will be alright. Perhaps we will. Inch by inch the shore comes closer. Another foot, another yard. The wind howls and lightning strikes somewhere on the forested shore. I count the seconds till the next thunder crash. Five seconds. Does that mean the storm is moving away? That old formula, dredged up from childhood, to take way the fears.

At last, at last, we reach the shore. It's pouring with rain. My legs are shaking so much I can hardly get out of the boat. Perversely, I get the giggles. I have never been so glad to be on dry land in my life. I would actually kneel down and kiss the mud if it weren't so theatrical. While Sharma pays the boatman, I look back over the lake. The distant island has vanished beyond a wall of rain, as though it had never been.

We sprint up the beach, through the deluge. Sharma waves down a taxi on the main road and we fling ourselves wetly into it.

The taxi driver drives like a maniac along the lake road, but I don't care. He takes in a detour to pick up a couple of his mates. They jam in the back with Sharma. When we get back he tries to overcharge us 20 rupees. Sharma refuses to let me pay the extra. It is the first time I have seen Sharma angry. He lectures the taxi driver on the virtues of honesty. The tourists, he says (simultaneously translating for me) are 'in our care'. This does not go down well with the spivvy driver who screeches round in a temper, almost running over Sharma's foot. He buckets off over the potholes, setting the fluffy dice in the back window dancing viciously.

It occurs to me that Sharma may be a bit stressed. We walk together through the hotel gate. It's still raining slightly. I remember that we are supposed to be going out for dinner in an hour and I look like a drowned rat. On the hotel steps, I turn to face Sharma, who is standing soaked to the skin, in short sleeves. After the altercation with the taxi driver, he is calm once again.

'It was a wonderful day. I loved the butterflies. And thanks for reassuring me on the lake. I'm such a coward!'

He grins, a trifle ruefully, and shakes his head.

'Actually,' he says after a moment, 'I can't swim.'

18

I am awake at four a.m. after deep contented sleep (and hang the dogs). Beyond my window, it's dim and pale before dawn. I struggle into warm gear, feverish not to miss a moment, and race onto the roof – no one. It is as empty as a bell jar.

The holy mountain hangs clear, with the whole Annapurna range behind. A flush of dawn comes up before the sun. I witness, all alone, one of the most fantastic sights on earth; the unseen sun touching the first tops to rose and gold as the highest peaks on earth are brushed with first light, springing into fire.

Tears run down my cheeks as, with my hands on the concrete balcony, I stand in the great church of the world in awe. After yesterday's storm, the sky is ringing with brightness. Other people are behind me now, but I have had this gift, all alone, in one miraculous moment of life.

We are taken out beyond Pokhara to the east, on this perfect day. I look on it all with great affection – the street crowds, the mangy dogs, children waving on their way to school. The open-fronted shops have a colour and warmth I hadn't seen before. Out of town, down a rutty road, there are beehive haystacks, women walking with *dokos*. Beside the lake shore there are pink houses beside the road, vegetable gardens and goats. It is a dear familiar scene. Everything is gilded with some indefinable joy.

On the trail the heat doesn't bother me. I can stride out strongly, fit after days of walking and a strict vegetarian diet. The trail is steep from the beginning. A half-grown girl and her smaller brother walk with me towards their school on the hill, wearing their smart blue blouses. They point to their hut, hanging on the valley side. For a couple of miles we have our usual puffed-out conversation (me, not them). I play back their questions on the micro-recorder and we giggle together.

The girl has a smooth shining plait. Every question is

preceded by *'Madam, please'*. They want me to come to their school, which is over there, off the main trail. I explain I can't today. They want to write to me. Half a dozen more girls appear from nowhere. I transcribe my address in an exercise book with a fountain pen which one of them proudly lends me. 'No, I can't write any more. I'll get left behind.'

After a bit Sue drops back to walk with me. We wander on through the dappled shade, past goats browsing, in a dried-up river bed. Presumably in the monsoon, this is a rushing torrent, but just now there is vegetation on the steep sandy banks, and coniferous woodland above. An enclosed world, shady and cool, made cooler by the watery song of the bulbul somewhere in the woods.

We have come to a fork in the track, and we have no idea which way the others have gone. We ask an old man with goats which way the English trekkers went, and he points to the steep track, so we hurry on. At last we catch up with the rest as they are taking a breather. All at once we are high. The trees fall back. Before us is brilliant azure sky and perfect mountains. Not a cloud in sight. We climb and climb in the heat, but I am no longer enervated by it, even when I get out of breath, which is still quite often. I can overtake the others, relishing the feel of my legs, and I feel so well, I could go on walking for ever. Now I am ready to go higher still, up into that mysterious country behind the Fishtail, high into the snows. I *can* do it now, I feel so strong.

We stop for a while, near lunchtime, by a high wall which seems to divide the mountain pasture from the lower slopes, like the stone walls in Cumbria but higher. It is the nearest we will get to the great snow-covered peaks for now. We are all very quiet, except Clive and Mavis. The power of these great mountains shines down on us, illuminating everything. We are so near to this blazing whiteness that we can see every glacier and arête.

Sharma comes up beside me. Handing me the binoculars, he

points out a pink house under the last foothills before the snows begin. There is a circle over the door, enclosing two crossed kukri. A Ghurkha house.

Glen takes pictures of us all. Adrian, who hopes to come back to climb, takes out his map of the joined-up mountains. Standing by the wall with the map before him, he instructs us in the names of all the peaks and glaciers, from West to East. Furthest over to the right we can just glimpse Dhaulagiri, once thought to be the world's highest mountain. It peers out from beyond Annapurna South Face. Then there is Annapurna I, Machhapuchhare, utterly dominating the sky, Annapurna III, Annapurna IV and Annapurna II.

After a bit, I can't bear to be with the others. I climb higher to the limit of the wall, and stand there for a long time. The power of these mountains washes over me. They are so high it is beyond understanding. Untameable. I don't really want to know their names. Men and women can walk on them, struggle up them, sweat and defecate on them, spoil the whiteness of their snows, but at the end of the day these mountains will never be tamed. The wisest mountaineers, often the greatest in their field, know that well. I think of Sherpa Tensing on the 1953 Everest expedition, getting down on his knees to beg forgiveness from Chomolungma, Mother Goddess of the World, for disturbing her peace.

The holiness is there, so powerful we have all sensed it. It 'speaks to our condition', going beyond the clutter of our lives. The more we are here, the more our ears can hear the singing of the world, and the more we are humbled by our smallness.

I remember the first time I was a 'body' for the Mountain Rescue Search Dogs, when I was writing one of my books, lying out in the snow at the back of Skiddaw, looking over the white fells. I felt the power of mountains for the first time then, lying against the rock for hours by a waterfall. But that was a whisper compared to this. This is a great shout. The *OM* vibration. The very essence of what I am. Its power beats down on me.

I remember those words of Sir John Hunt's Sherpa, a few months before he died. *'We are the blood and the mountains are our bones.'*

'Om Mani Padme Hum.' The Jewel in the Heart of the Lotus. *Om,* among the gods: *Ma* in the world of Titans and spirits: *Ni,* in the human world: *Pad,* in the world of animals: *Me* as a Tantalus in the world of ghosts: *Hum,* in the depths of Hell.

So here it is, laid out before me. In the foreground, on the cropped pasture, minute blue flowers, half the size of a little fingernail, tiny alpine gentians scattered among clumps of sheep or goat dung. Smaller insects struggle over blue flowers and stunted grass. My senses are so sharpened that I see it all as though through a microscope, with a profound, intense reality.

'Heaven in a (white) flower; the Universe in a grain of sand.'

The wall glows in sharp oranges and blues in this unearthly crystal light, and beyond forested slopes fold into another and another. A few miles and the snows begin. I am almost there, touching the snow at the base of the Holy Mountain. The Abode of the Gods.

I look down on the others, my eyes blurred with tears. I seem to see into everything, as though, just for once in my life, I am in tune with something deeper. Because I have stopped for long enough. Because I have listened. Because I have been still.

To my horror, through my tears, I see Mavis making her purposeful way up to me. She climbs steadily, a set look on her face. All the other are looking now. They know why I wanted to be alone. She stops beside me and leans on the wall, breathless and confidential. I try to cover what I have been writing, surreptitiously wiping my eyes.

'I thought I would come up and have a word,' she says at last, when she has got her breath back. 'You've been up here such a long time, I thought the view must be better!'

She looks away over the foothills towards the blazing glory of

Machhapuchhare. Does she too feel what I feel, here?

'Well,' she says at last. 'It seems to be much the same. I think I'll go on down if you don't mind.'

We climb on for another half hour or so, till we get to a village, just one street. There is a long modern building at the far end, a teahouse with a veranda. It isn't a nice village like the one we stopped at the day we came over on the lake. All is soon explained. It is the local guide's aunty who runs the tea house, so we all have to spend an hour here, surrounded by flies and stinks. The whole village decamps from their houses to say 'hello'. It's impossible to move for people crowding round and staring.

We sit on the steps of the veranda, and at the couple of dusty wooden tables and chairs, laid out for customers in the middle of the street. Sue, with the precision of a surgeon performing a life-saving operation, lays out a pristine knife, a miniature box of Boots Slimmers pâté and a couple of slices of crisp bread wrapped in cling film, on a tissue on the table. We get the giggles as she tries to spread the pâté on the crisp bread without touching anything.

I buy a very hot Coke from the box which has been standing in the sun, rather than the cool stuff which is standing in a bucket of water. It is a toss-up which is less dodgy – the bottle which has been standing in the street encrusted in dust, or the bottle which is covered in slimy water from the bucket. I wipe the top gingerly and get out one of my last straws, bent and misshapen after days in a rucksack. In my confusion, I drop my Leki stick on the ground, in something human or animal. I am back in the real world, the one where I am always in a muddle, not the world of poetry and dream where I am almost a dancer.

Sue, meanwhile, cool and efficient, is munching away at her Boots pâté, while half the male adolescent population of the village stare at her from a foot or two away. She looks wonderful, even in her old purple tracksuit. I'm rather grumpy and have a whinge to Annabel about having to stop in this village for lunch. This is a hazard of having a local guide whose relatives all seem to run teahouses. I have never known such flies, and it is very hot.

I am desperate for the loo and go off in search of a private spot away from the village. First of all, I find myself in what is obviously the village squatting place, complete with vast amount of evidence. I can't face it, especially as a number of small black pigs are rooting about in the remains. I am being followed by four little girls who want to hold my hand and practise their English, and the rest of the secondary school pupils (apart from those who are in the village staring at Sue) are leaning over the wall on the far side of the track, shouting 'GOOD MORNING, MADAM. ARE YOU ENGLISH PLEASE?' I decide to take the main trail upwards out of the village. I climb on and on. This is a rather straggling village with more new building on the outskirts, ugly concrete, much of the time. It must be prosperous. Going down a rocky cul de sac, I surprise a man with a water buffalo, as I am about to take my chance. It's no good. There are people everywhere.

On the way back down, still busting, a very old woman beckons to me to sit with her, patting the stone beside her. It is the first time I have been directly approached. I smile and try to indicate that I have to get back. If it weren't for my real discomfort, and the worry about missing the others, I would stop for a little while. An opportunity missed for ever. And half of me is still afraid of crossing another bridge. Further down, a young woman comes out of her doorway, a baby in her arms. She calls to me.

'Are you going far, sister? Are you on the trail?'

It is as though while I have been part of a group I was invisible, or maybe the women are too shy to approach. But as soon as I am on my own, it's different. I feel part of it all again.

The woman with the baby goes on asking me things.

'Do you have a man? Where do you live? Do you have children?' She has really good English, and is very curious about me, not shy at all. I explain that my group is in the village. I have to go. I leave our conversation regretfully. More and more, I am beginning to feel the inadequacy of being part of a group. It isolates me from that underlife I sense but can only experience a little, tantalisingly out of reach. I will have to come back again, alone, to explore that strange sense of belonging. To stand under those perfect mountains. Will I have the courage?

The others are waiting, ready to leave. I follow them out of the village. The old woman is still sitting outside her house on the wall, but this time she doesn't call to me. I am beyond her reach, and she beyond mine.

We trudge on upwards in the heat. This is the highest we have gone so far. Everyone stops at one point, in an empty landscape with two trees, a wall and a distant house. It's dry and dusty and the lushness of the valleys has disappeared. The deforestation we have heard about everywhere.

Two women, swathed in brilliant fuchsia tops, labour up the track towards us, heavily laden *dokos* filled with leaves on their backs, cigarettes hanging from their mouths. Devra Murphy, in her book, *The Waiting Land*, writes about the cigarette as the curse and the consolation of the Nepalese people. La'al, our local guide, lights up whenever we stop and the young lads in the villages are usually puffing away. Sharma doesn't smoke.

We begin to walk eastwards, following another higher wall. Two tiny girls in pink jumpers and skirts prance along beside us. Up here it is bare, the soil thin and dry, just the odd tree. A water buffalo, half-starved, wanders past us with her calf in search of grass. There are scarred patches where felling has been going on. As we reach the bare hillside above a village, we can see rows of newly planted deciduous saplings, which may be part of the Annapurna Project, a village-centred scheme designed to be run by villagers themselves, re-foresting areas, which have been hardest hit by deforestation.

It's mid-afternoon when we reach another, even higher stretch of pasture, the two little girls still trailing along with us. A group of women with children are having a picnic on the hillside. They smile and say *Namaste!* and we stop for a while. Sharma sits cross-legged on the grass a little way away, his eyes closed. One or two of us climb a little higher to be away from the others. On the top of this hill is a stone water tank like the one in the sadhu's sanctuary. When the monsoon comes, this will store water for the houses down the hillside. Butterflies dance around in pairs. The great mountains hang in the sky, a little more distant now, yet I can still feel their power. Because we are higher, the air has that alpine coolness like fell tops in summer, though we must be several times the height of any fell.

Sharma is down on the pasture, still cross-legged, with his eyes closed, but Clive is getting restless. He doesn't like too much silence. He goes down to Sharma, snapping his fingers in front of his eyes. Everyone is looking. Watching from above, I am outraged. Sharma, infinitely peaceful, opens his eyes and smiles. As though speaking to some coolie on a 1920's expedition, Clive instructs him that he wishes to record the children who are gathered nearby, part of the village picnic. Would Sharma please get them together? Then to demonstrate his skill with his tape recorder, he plays his last recording at full blast, the limpid, crystal silence of this high place shattered by the tinny sound. We look at each other and one by one turn away, unable to bear it. How can we face Sharma again? Yet he is laughing, and by now, Clive is too late. The picnic party has packed up and is moving down the hill. Serves him right. Clive stalks off. Sharma returns to his meditation.

The hillside returns to its silence. I sit, utterly at peace, deep in a spell again. The village squatting place, pigs and flies, interruptions and irritations, sensitive and insensitive tourists, absent-minded middle-aged women with too much emotional baggage, Buddhist monks with serenity like a cloak around them, the women of the tribes, beggars on the street, saints and thieves, all exist within this deep enchantment, this sacred life which shines down from the mountains. All things exist side by side. There is no conflict. Each is part of the other. The vibration of life, the great *OM*, is in everything. It weaves the world into a seamless fabric. Molecules sing in the universe. And in this place, we are as close to hearing that song as anywhere on earth.

I sit a little longer, under these shining snows, trying to hold that in my being. The butterflies dance in front of me, around the stone water tank. I could reach out my hands and catch them. I could hold them and look at them, but that fragile, glowing colour would turn to dust in my hands. I let them fly away.

19

Suddenly it's all over. We are back in Kathmandu, among the traffic, the horns, the swell of people. Even from my window, high up, the mountains are invisible. Time to go home.

Sharma has melted away. After saying goodbye to Annabel, his job of guiding this little party of walkers is over. No doubt he is exhausted.

I feel fitter than I have been for years. An examination of myself in the mirror shows that I have lost a lot of weight – all that staggering up trekking paths in the heat. How come I feel so – unfinished? So lost at the thought of going home? It is terribly disloyal. I want to see my family, yet on this last day there is a strange sadness. It wells up in me. As soon as I get back to my room – the same room – I stand under the creaky shower for what seemed like hours, but I can't wash this feeling away.

We fly tomorrow morning. We have just this last day in Nepal. Directionless, we sit about in the courtyard, talking desultorily. I feel I should go into Kathmandu, see something, do something. What am I waiting for – sitting here in the sun?

I ring home to tell them that I had arrived back safely, but the kids are watching *Neighbours* and don't seem very interested. Dad is out with the dogs. No messages. I have a sudden feeling of a self-sufficient world back there without me. It is something I will become familiar with – culture shock in reverse.

I go down to the hotel lobby and stand looking out of the door at the dusty street. There is a soft voice behind me.

'*Namaste*, Angela.' Sharma is standing there, smiling his smile, his hands together. 'I need you to come with me.'

So I go – trustingly, like a shot through the doorway, Sharma walking fast. I struggle to keep up with him, plunging into the tumultuous world of the market in Thamel – noise, colour, scent, stenches, heaving bodies, shop signs everywhere, a tangle of

wires above the narrow streets. On and on, it seems like miles.
Then a little shop on a corner which just sells necklaces. We go
into the airless space. Everything sparkles.

'Please. Choose one. It's for you.'

I'm overwhelmed.

'Because you are my friend.'

One beautiful necklace shimmers in the corner, every
iridescent colour of blue from indigo to the colour of the sky at
dawn.

'That one! It reminds me of the butterflies in the garden of the
Fishtail Lodge.'

He is happy. It is given to me. It shimmers against my skin.

Once again, at breakneck speed, we thread, push, skirt, barge
through the crowds in Thamel. I am wearing my beautiful
necklace. Outside the hotel, Sharma stops.

He places his hands outside mine.

'You must come back. To finish what you have started.'

'Yes, I will. I promise.'

'Then I will be your guide. I will show you what needs to be
done.'

This is a promise between us. I will not forget.

I cry all the way home, especially as we take off and see those
pink, dusty fields below us, the bruise of pollution on the horizon.
And then again, at Frankfurt Airport when we change planes, I
stand weeping helplessly. It is all too much. The gold-plated tape
recorders, the solid gold lighters, the huge televisions on sale in
duty-free. Too much. Too awful. Too obscene. I have been with
people who have nothing, and they have given me everything. I
weep, remembering the girl who cleaned my room. When we came
back, she had knocked on my door in the morning.

'Miss, you left your earrings under the pillow when you went
away. I find them. I save them for you.' She has a baby, a sick
husband, but would like to study. Story after story. Need after
need. So impossible.

20

I am not a success. Coming home. No doubt they are glad to see me, give me hugs, but it's different for them too. Dad has put up big lists of jobs in the kitchen and everyone has to do them. How does he manage that? They will never do anything for me. In my absence, they have bonded into a tight little team. I am redundant, and I feel excluded. Unfairly, since it was I who went away, I want them to want me back, but I have changed forever.

My behaviour doesn't help. I seem alien, distracted, almost mad. When the children whine about not having mountain bikes for Christmas, I leap out of the bath, naked and furious.

'You don't know how lucky you are! I have been with people who have nothing!'

I am insufferable, ranting like an Old Testament prophet. My children are as compassionate as any. It's just that they haven't been there yet, to see for themselves.

As for their father, the poor man is all at sea. And so am I. Somehow, we cling on, staring across a gulf between what has happened to me and what has *not* happened to him. Then I announce my intention of going back – borrowing the money from the bank, paying it back through supply teaching. This doesn't go down too well. Why should it? We are speaking a different language.

'Have you been taking drugs?' My husband asks one night, in despair. 'You are so different.'

I am on the other side of a glass wall, shouting back into my old world. And no one can hear.

I keep in touch with my old walking companions. Several of them are experiencing similar symptoms – especially Glen (who ends up working with disabled children in Bhaktapur). Much later, I will see the effect of returning into this old world on the young volunteers. The culture shock is in the coming back. No one prepares you for it. At last, in despair, I seek out my friendly doctor.

'I think I'm going mad,' I tell him. 'I can't settle. The shock of being back in the West, after all I have seen, is just too much. And no one,' I bleat pathetically, 'seems to understand!'

He listens, and then tells me about his own father, coming back to his family after his first visit to Africa, finding it impossible to go back to his old life.

'Do something about it,' he counsels. 'It might help.'

At the school which I have returned to (after having leave of absence) they have a project in Malawi and enough on their plates raising money for that. I drive up into the fells to visit the regional head of one of the big charities. It is the only mega-charity, I have heard, which is truly effective in Nepal. I arrive there at the same time as a young couple, photographers, who have also just got back. They want to set up an exhibition in aid of some of the charity's projects. Not interested. We are all sent away crushed. Despite our zeal, we have nothing to offer.

'Leave it to the professionals,' is his advice. I will hear that phrase over and over again. And it's true! Yet, from what I have understood, the professional bodies, by and large, hardly leave Kathmandu valley. Money swills about, rarely reaching into the hinterland. Without a strong local and national structure reaching into the hill villages and hardly any roads, it is difficult to help those who may be in need. But what *is* the need? There is so much malnutrition and high infant mortality. Diseases, such as smallpox, supposedly eradicated by WHO programmes, sometimes resurface. Deaths from water-borne diseases – amoebic dysentery, cholera – are common, as is typhoid. Even the higher reaches of rivers in Nepal are polluted by the use of village latrines. Millions of pounds and dollars pour into Nepal. Yet, by some indicators, the country has the worst record for misappropriating Aid in the Developing World.

Why try to fix anything? Aren't we in the West just being

arrogant? We with our Western ways have already brought dental caries (*Give me one sweet!*) and other Western diseases. We trek, cause deforestation (hot showers in tea houses) and bring in tourist dollars which fuel, not immunisation programmes, not Health Education in the hills, but men who stand on street corners in leather jackets and sunglasses talking into their mobile phones – a new, Aid-funded middle class.

Sharma's voice comes back to me. 'We need small things. Start small. Do it well.'

I phone an acquaintance in the city, a millionaire, part of my now distant life before we moved to Cumbria. Put through to one of his assistants, I leave a message and I am eventually contacted by his P.A. I explain passionately that I am trying to set up a small-scale Educational link with Nepal. Hopefully, it will be of mutual benefit and crucially, has been requested by the Nepalese themselves. It would involve taking out books and resource materials to Dhulikhel and building a new, much-needed classroom in the earthquake-damaged school down the hill. The smooth Sloaney-voiced P.A. listens patiently. Then there is a pause.

'The thing is,' she says at last, 'It's frightfully awkward, but X only gives to charities where the Princess of Wales is involved.' So you get invited to the Charity Ball, I think to myself, remembering how much X always made of his philanthropic work. 'My advice,' says Miss Sloane, 'is leave it to the professionals. *They* know what they are doing.'

I put the phone down, stung to tears. She's right, of course. But also, sometimes, wrong. Now I know that, shockingly, much Aid is wasted, used as a political tool, that paid professionals often get it horribly wrong too. The other side of the coin is that time after time, little people, insignificant people, have gone out on a limb for a country they care passionately about, and occasionally they can make a disproportionately big difference. Sometimes too, of course, they cause a lot of damage and ill-feeling. And there are many wonderful, dedicated professional charity workers in the larger charities whose main currency is simply love – not money, but care, attention, involvement, listening. But big is not *necessarily* beautiful. The Schumacher Principle applies universally – 'Small *is* beautiful'.

For now, I am very discouraged. One man I greatly respect, who taught for years in Papau New Guinea, reinforces the official advice, 'All Aid is bad.' I am shocked into silence.

The phone rings. It's Harriet's school, Ullswater Community College in Penrith, where I have chatted to some of the staff about my trip over the past weeks. Would I come in and give a talk to a Year group?

It goes unexpectedly well. I find myself talking with passion and something of what I am trying to say gets across. The kids, young teenagers, are absorbed. My slides seem to glow with colour and life. It is a powerful experience to relive my time in Nepal. I find myself once again close to tears. Afterwards a couple of the staff, Maggie and Shaun, come up to me and tell me they have decided to run a school trip to Nepal for the Year group next year. They want the kids to get a sense of the country, some understanding, and crucially, to get involved in a project to benefit Nepal. The children will have to raise their own funding for the trip and for a chosen project. I had told the group about the earthquake-damaged school. They would like to send money in advance to build a classroom.

This is the first time anything positive has come out of all the photocopying of letters, all those phone calls. The first time I haven't come up against a brick wall. The kids are so enthusiastic, crowding round and asking questions. I tell them I am going back in October by myself. They tell me that by then they will have raised enough money for a new classroom, by screen washing and bag packing at the local supermarket. Could I take some money out with me?

Numerous faxes later, I have fixed my trip through Sharma's

trekking company and all the arrangements have been made. I have given up my job. I will go back on the supply list on my return, so that I can pay back my trip money. All I have to do now is face saying goodbye to my family and deal with all those conflicting emotions.

My husband takes me down to Heathrow in the evening, and I have to leave him. It's October and already dark outside. This time there are no other members of the party. Just me. The Royal Nepal Airlines plane is due to leave at 7.30. After overseeing the embarrassing scene at the check-in (my bag is, as usual, too heavy, and I have to take rather a lot of stuff out) Colin sees me through the gate. He gives me a long hug.

'I don't know how I can let you go on your own. You look so small.'

I am close to tears, frightened, and with a strong sense of doing something very foolish.

'I'll be fine.'

The plane is delayed for two hours. I am alone in the departure lounge, watching *Songs of Praise* on TV. Oddly, it is coming from the Lake District. Recorded in early summer – trees in blossom, a shining lake - Sir Chris Bonington is being interviewed. He and his wife Wendy have been among the people who encouraged me to come out to Nepal. Together with Martha Scott, Doug Scott's daughter, they had made me feel that what I was dreaming of doing was not entirely insane, might even be achievable. Chris and Wendy, and Doug and his first wife, Jan, were close neighbours of ours at the time in North Cumbria.

Somehow, in that dimly-lit departure lounge, black night beyond the windows, the sight of Sir Chris on *Songs of Praise*, gives my spirit a much-needed lift, before the long flight ahead.

21

We sink slowly between the jagged mountains. The sight of those brown hills, that smoky pollution in the valley, is not inspiring.

After the horrors of customs, dizzy and exhausted from lack of sleep, a familiar face awaits me. Sharma hasn't let me down. In a navy blazer and sparkling white shirt, his face wreathed in smiles, he has arranged everything, including a taxi to my hotel. As we drive through Kathmandu, those familiar smells and sights assail me powerfully – orange, dusky light, dust, dirt, noise, a combination of human and animal dung, building works and red diesel fumes, the indefinable smell of Kathmandu. It is so evocative that my heart swells. I feel, mysteriously, I have come home.

The next morning we are due to go up to Dhulikhel and the true journey will begin. I have no way of knowing that Nepal this time would give me almost more happiness than I can bear, and some of the worst moments of my life. It will change me as the previous journey has, in ways that I can't yet imagine.

In Dhulikhel, the sun beats down on the school roof. A group of town dignitaries have assembled to receive the donation from Ullswater Community College. I have arrived with six hundred dollars secreted around my body, enough to build a classroom. It's a beginning. I pass on letters from Ullswater, explaining that they hope to come out for a project visit the following year. They will be in touch directly with Sanjiwani Upper Secondary School, who will be their 'partners'. Once again, there is a sense of beginning.

The following morning, there is a knock on my door before dawn. Sharma has come to wake me so that I could watch the sunrise over the Himalayas again. In the pre-dawn chill, we walk up the steep, sandy trail to the viewpoint. All around us is a low-growing shrub with needle-like leaves, dark against the pale path. A strangely familiar scent hangs in the misty air, reminding me, oddly, of the Lake District.

The sky is getting lighter, but the sun had not yet broken through. Suddenly, on the trail beside me, a tiny girl is matching my steps in her flip-flops. In a light *lunghi* and a strappy vest, her hair wild, face encrusted with the evidence of the upper respiratory diseases to which Nepalese children are prone, she offers me her hand and walks beside me, coughing at every step, and shivering in the morning chill.

Sharma is walking behind us. When we get to the viewpoint the sun is about to rise over the mountains. I remember that last time, when I stood here on this mountainside in a tangle of cameras, trying to capture the moment. Will it be the same again?

The little girl is still shivering.

'How do you say in Nepalese, *Are you feeling cold?*' I ask Sharma.

He tells me. I repeat, 'Kai Timilai Jado Cha?'

The little girl looks up at me, 'Jado Cha,' she says, shivering. *I am cold*.

As usual either over-dressed or under-dressed, I haven't even brought a sweater or coat with me to lend her against the morning chill. She lets go of my hand and runs off into the green undergrowth. Below the trail, I can see a hut perched on the edge of a tiny rice field, the smoke and the first fire of the morning, curling up into the still sky. This must be where she lives. A few moments later the little girl returns, holding some dark green leaves in her hand. She speaks to me in Nepalese, but I don't understand. My language has run out. She rubs the leaves vigorously, holding her hands under my nose. An aromatic scent drifts up on the still air.

'Because you spoke to her in her language, she wishes to give you a gift,' Sharma translates. 'This is Juniper from her valley.'

That fragrant scent which pervades the air, and was so was

familiar! It takes me back to my own place in Cumbria, the valley in the North Lakes where Juniper grows, a rare last remnant of the Ice Age. Both of us, fleeting friends, the little girl and I, share in that moment a gift of memory and delight, which has transported me between mountain and mountain, from one side of the world to another.

Together, hand in hand, we watch the sun rise into a clear sky. Beyond the mist which lies in the valley, beyond the black crows flying across from hill to hill, the distant smoke of fires, are those shining mountains lit to pale rose and gold by the rising sun. The little girl holds my hand tightly. Then we walk down to where her mother, in an orange sari, waits for her outside her hut. Suddenly she is gone, away down the trail, turning once to smile her gappy smile, before disappearing into the dark doorway. In silence, Sharma and I walk together down the trail. There is no need for words.

It will be a long time before I realise the full significance of the gift from the little girl. Juniper is the sacred herb of Buddhists, used for holy ceremonies, for the cleansing of the spirit. A gift beyond price, one that I will never forget. Somehow, mysteriously, it will bind me for ever to this country and its beautiful people.

22

We cram into the bus on the way down to Kathmandu Valley. Perhaps it's just jet lag catching up with me, but I am beginning to feel very strange. By the time I get to my little hotel, I am running a raging temperature, which the forehead thermometer tells me it is 103F. I have a raging sore throat. Within two hours, I am really ill.

I ring home in a panic. It is pre-dawn there. Kathmandu is five and a half hours ahead. A grumpy voice answers, half-asleep, not in the best of tempers. Can he find my medical insurance?

Things get worse. EuropAssistance appears in the hotel. How bizarre! They make a fuss and insist I have extra blankets. Since I have arrived back we have been plagued with power cuts, and the hotel in late November is freezing cold. My temperature continues to mount, and looking at myself in the mirror, my throat seems to be closing up. Once again, I feel very alone.

Sharma comes to visit.

'Don't go into hospital', he says, looking worried. 'If the doctor comes, don't let them take you into hospital. It's a terrible place, full of lepers.'

Surely it won't come to that?

The doctor arrives, a handsome, aristocratic Nepali with a bored bedside manner. The cost of the visit, 60 dollars, would be a fortune in Nepal. He diagnoses an 'unknown virus' and prescribes antibiotics. Sharma comes back and offers to get the prescriptions and whatever else I need. Even though I am not booked in to the hotel beyond the next morning, they will still take care of me. They will consider it an honour, he explains.

For four days I lie in the hotel with a fever. The spicy Nepalese food is inedible with my swollen throat. All I can do is drink bottled water and gargle with Disprin. At night, in the lonely hours, I look down my throat, seeing the hole between my non-existent tonsils getting smaller and smaller. Thank goodness, at the time I didn't know that my own youngest daughter would soon be diagnosed twice with quinsy and have to be rushed into hospital. Is this the backbone that created Empire? Not in this case! I am seriously frightened. Typhoid, diphtheria, any number of unimaginable diseases – despite the injections – all possibilities chase across my fevered mind.

Sharma comes several times a day with supplies of tissues in tiny boxes, all that's available in Kathmandu, Disprin and antibiotics, water, little plates of food which I can't eat. However, thankfully, I begin to recover, and eventually we are able to rearrange our trip to Pokhara. Sharma has been a tower of strength, certainly preventing my having to go into hospital.

A basket of flowers sent up from Housekeeping - those kindly, loving souls who had kept me going with endless lemon drinks in the middle of the night - *'Thank you for the honour of being able to look after you'*. I leave the isolation of my hotel room for the stinks of Kathmandhu with bizarre regret. In that room, I have been able to look out of the window at the life of Kathmandu; the little café below my window where trekkers come for breakfast; Kali, the protecting deity, on the Nawari carving above my window, where pigeons roost, cooing softly; the distant sight of hills behind the mist; the old man in the square below wrapped in his muffler, coughing and shivering over a brazier in the foggy morning air.

'You have taken care of me so well,' I say to Sharma. 'Can I give you something, a gift to tell you how much I appreciate all you have done?'

He thinks for a moment.

'I don't need anything, but my wife's school is very poor. Would you come and see? They need clean water. The children get sick from dirty water. So do the teachers! Even my wife gets sick and she's used to Kathmandu.' He smiles his peaceful smile.

'If you wish to give me a gift, you could give clean water to the children and the teachers. Perhaps you could donate a water tank? I would like that very much.' So it's agreed.

For the first time in a week I am outside in the 'fresh' air, actually so polluted you could be asphyxiated just crossing the road. That is, of course, if you weren't run over first. The dust hangs, a potent mix of red diesel belched out by every home-made tractor and every 'tuc-tuc', mingling with the aromatic dung of free-wandering sacred cows, lorries on the road up from India, spices, unwashed bodies, the air-borne tapestry of the streets...

We travel down through Kathmandu to meet Sharma's wife, Sita – a long walk in the dusk down shadowy paths on the outskirts of town, dim figures brushing past – until we reach the modern, brick-built house on a little development. Concrete stairs, and steel rods stick out of the roof-space ready for another storey to be built. The whole of 'new' Kathmandu is like this – a building site never finished, room to expand as more children arrive, and perhaps if the house is never finished, there will be less tax to pay? Sharma's house is the height of luxury, electric lights in pretty wall lamps, three storeys, a flush toilet and western-style shower, not just the ubiquitous rubber pipe sticking out of the wall for intimate ablutions. But Sharma laughs. The shower doesn't work 'yet' and he washes every morning with a bucket of water.

Sita is waiting for us, beautiful, her face full of laughter. She makes a big fuss of me, an honoured guest, and gives me rakshi she has brewed herself. She is one of a high-born tribe who are allowed to do this. The pure spirit is poured from an ornate brass jug with a long spout, her arm uplifted as she stands. Though she is giggling the whole time, she manages to fill a tiny brass cup on the table from a distance of three feet. This ceremony is her way of honouring a guest. The rakshi courses down my oesophagus and into my veins like liquid fire. She presses more on me and little cakes in an ornate dish. Sharma stands and smiles at us both. After the rakshi, Sita insists on dressing me in one of her saris, laughing all the while. I am wearing the necklace Sharma gave me. He takes my picture, enshrined forever as an honorary Nepali. The ceremony is both solemn and hilarious, with that mixture of laughter and holiness which is uniquely Nepalese.

We agree to go to Sita's school the next day and I leave with Sharma, who is going to escort me back to the hotel. Sita speaks no English at all but we have managed to communicate happily all evening. As I go, she gives me a hug.

We walk back down the pitch-black, narrow paths. No lights, just a sensation of people brushing past in a hurry, going somewhere, to work or away from work. Women shrouded in scarves against the chill.

'Nepalese women work very hard!' Sharma whispers.

I am glad Sharma is with me. I would never find my way back on my own through this maze of paths in the dark. Out on the main road, he hails a tuc-tuc and we bump along in companionable silence till we get to my hotel.

'My wife likes you very much,' he says, as he climbs back into the tuc-tuc on his way home.

'I like her too!' It seems inadequate.

Alone in my room, I reluctantly change back out of my sari, which Sita has insisted on presenting to me as a gift. Wearing it, I had a sense of being initiated, welcomed even, into something profound and new. And there is a warm feeling of belonging.

Next day, it's on to Sita's school in Patan – iron bars on the windows, hands reaching out, blue blouses, pleated skirts, noise and dust. The bars are shocking, like cattle pens. Beyond the brilliant light of the sandy yard, are the reaching hands, the smiling faces of children. The interiors of the classrooms are very dark.

The headmistress is wearing a posh sari, bouffant western hair. Sita is laughing in the background. Everything is fun to her.

I am taken across the playground through wildly excited children who want to hold my hands. This is where the water tank will be, clean water to be delivered by tanker once a week.

'No more diarrhoea. Teachers – no! Children – no!'

Everyone smiles. They promise they will send me a receipt for the water tank and a photograph. Every gift in Nepal, even money given in the hills for a school, is received with a conscientious receipt (in more recent times, even some Maoist rebels, after relieving trekkers of cameras and money, have provided a receipt in exchange).

Fifteen years later, that water tank still stands in the corner of the school, with *Angela Locke of Scotland* written on its top. I had explained that I live in the Borders. The tank has now been joined by two others from Juniper Trust, and by toilets and running water, and remains one of the most useful gifts I have ever been able to give anybody.

For now, it's time to fly up to Pokhara in a tiny plane. I have a touch of 'Kathmandu Quickstep', despite my neurotic hand-washing and a strict vegetarian diet, and look for a loo in the airport. It's pitch black in the lavatories and I can see nothing, only smell the stench. I hope I am going in the right place. On the way out, a woman at the gate looks at me reproachfully. She has removed the light bulb. There is a box containing rupees – a bribe for her to put the light bulb back. Too late! I wish I had noticed before I stepped in something unspeakable.

Small plane. The hostess crawls down the aisle on her hands and knees with peanuts and drinks. It's beautiful flying low above forested slopes of hills, the plane's small shadow below us flitting above the endless green of juniper and rhododendron, unbroken by clearings – truly wild, with no paths between villages. It's been a beautiful day, until, on the right-hand horizon I spot a boil of cloud, very distant, a strange blackish-red colour. It's odd-looking, like a violent sunset, yet it's still early afternoon.

I watch the strange cloud scud across the sky with unbelievable speed. There is some time till we land. While the rest of the sky stays blue, this homunculus, a false sunset, stretches black fingers towards us from the distant mountains. Even here, in the plane, I can feel its chill.

Sharma is sitting in front of me. I tap him on the shoulder.

'Look.'

He has seen it already.

'Typhoon,' he says quietly. 'Don't worry. We should get there before.'

Should. Before.

The horrible boil of cloud, like a red cauldron, is travelling swiftly now across the previously innocent sky. The red eye of Sauron, radiating menace. We'll never get there before it hits. Looking down, the trees are as close-knit as a bear's coat. No place to land.

'How long till we get to Pokhara?'

'Fifteen minutes, maybe!'

Too long.

The carefree, rather pioneering spirit with which I undertook this journey has evaporated. I begin to pray. I think of the Dalai Lama, focus on his calm face on that postcard in my luggage.

By the time the hills above Pokhara come into view, almost the whole sky is black. The little plane is being buffeted about alarmingly. That red spot is now a full sunset, flying towards us. We start to descend. I try not to look at the way the wing is swinging up and down in the dark sky. Everyone on the plane is quiet. I stare at the back of Sharma's head, his close-curled black hair. He radiates stillness.

'Do not worry.'

A particularly violent lurch hits the plane, the engines sputtering. For long seconds we seem to fall without sound. There ahead is the dust track which is the runway. Falling. Another wild lurch. A mountain ahead. A small shack-like building I remember from last time. Rain hits the window with a crack.

The plane drops, hits earth. Thank God. We taxi to a halt. With unseemly haste, we are bundled out onto the small square of tarmac, just as a bolt of lightning strikes earth beyond the control tower. Simultaneously, the sky rains rocks. One hits me on the back of the head, another bruises my shoulder – huge hailstones crashing to earth. The wind is unbelievable, springing from nowhere like a tiger.

Sharma takes my arm.

'Run!'

Another crash as lightning strikes the ground ahead of us. We reach the airport building after what seems an age – soaked, frightened, while more lightning rakes the sky and the wind threatens to tear us off our feet. The pilot and the hostess, drenched, are running behind us. Behind them the plane, tiny and vulnerable, is tipped over at an angle. Our brave little plane has been holed by hailstones and blown over on one wing. What would have happened if we had still been in the air?

Through the glass doors, into the humid darkness of Arrivals. There has been a massive power cut, the whole of Pokhara. By the time our luggage is wrestled from the damaged plane, and we get out of the airport building, the typhoon has passed, off to wreak more damage in the hills. The streets, normally so dusty, are flooded a foot deep in muddy water, lapping at the edges of the wooden shop fronts. Thatched roofs of huts lie upended, in soaking clumps. There is a smell of burning flesh in the air. A water buffalo has been struck by lightning; a family now bereft of income. Everyone is subdued, clearing up debris.

***

I have given myself one night in Fishtail Lodge. The lakeshore is flooded and we have to wait, shivering, while the raft is rescued.

After my fright, it's so good to reach my thatched cabin set in the fragrant gardens. The sun comes out and the gardens fill with steam. The scent of flowers comes up to me in the clearing air. Mist rises from the lake. I am suddenly very tired, yet thankful to be alive in this intensely beautiful place. Here, as so often, life and death walk closely together.

***

Mist at dawn over the lake. It's cold. The mountains, white, distant, perfect, are reflected in this perfect mirror. A small boat, dream-like, drifts through the mist. An early fisherman. I have brought hibiscus blossom from the tree outside my cabin door, to float onto the lake. Sharma has been doing his morning practice, and now he comes to join me on the lake shore. He, too, places a hibiscus flower on the mirrored water. Together, the scented, glowing flowers waft in slow circles towards the mountains.

'Thankful time,' he says quietly.

23

'I have to show you something. It explains everything.'

On the outskirts of Pokhara a tin shed sits on a scruffy site on the edge of town. Row on row of looms are stacked through the long room. An occasional bird flies through; pigeon shit coats the machinery. All is silent, abandoned, except for the soft cooing of the pigeons and the clack of one loom working at the far end. There is an overwhelming sense of despair.

An emaciated woman, empty-eyed, weaves at a loom, backwards and forwards, backwards and forwards. Three tiny children, filthy, barefoot, play around her feet in the dirt, hiding in her skirts as we approach. She looks at us without hope. Skeletal hands moving through the machinery. Clack. Clack.

'TB,' whispers Sharma. He speaks softly to her and she answers in monosyllables, not pausing in her weaving. Clack, Clack, the sound reverberating through the empty shed.

'Big investment,' says Sharma. 'An American charity.'

'What happened?'

'Nothing happened. The shed got built, the looms were put in. No one asked the people if it was right. The looms broke. The materials ran out. There was no training.'

The woman looks at us with haunted, empty eyes in a skeletal face. Clack. Clack. Alone in a shed full of broken looms.

I won't forget this lesson.

We have more days in the hills, walking peacefully, learning more, meeting people and listening, before we fly back, thankfully without incident this time, to Kathmandu, and a warm welcome from Sita. There are a few days before I fly home. I have meetings with a few of the shakers and movers in Kathmandu – editors of liberal magazines, heads of small Nepalese charities, thinkers and educators. This is still a military dictatorship, and conversation is guarded. I appreciate I am being trusted. There is much frustration. Corruption, the abuse of international Aid, the unwillingness of some of the larger charities to leave Kathmandu valley and their comfortable 4 x 4's, the lack of any political will for any change... all this becomes shockingly clear, as I hear a catalogue of problems. I wish I had never begun.

A charming journalist asks me over lunch on the edge of Durbar Square:

'Do you know how often a team leaves Kathmandu for an immunisation programme? Twice a year on the King's and Queen's birthdays!'

Typhoid and cholera, borne by dirty water, and childhood diseases which kill children already under-nourished, all could be prevented. A nutrition programme for children – would it be workable? A few 'barefoot' Western doctors already carry vitamins and distribute them among the hill people. Save the Children do a lot, but basically outside Kathmandu – at that time, the early nineties – little medical help was provided, and there was no effective health programme, only individual charity initiatives, and a few small-scale operations, the shining exception being Everest climber Sir Edmund Hillary's Himalayan Trust, founded in 1960 to help the Sherpa people of the Khumbu in Nepal. Basic principles of working with communities in partnership, of all monies going straight to the source of need, of listening to the needs of local people, are seminally important and have influenced so many of us who want to help in our small way in Nepal.

Now, too, Everest mountaineer Doug Scott's innovative community project, Community Action Nepal (CAN) www.canepal.org., has built six Health Posts in the Middle Hills of Nepal and eight schools, and two porter rescue shelters near Everest. With clean water projects, they have put in over 40 projects altogether, all in close participation with the village people. Nepal Trust, too, sets up treks for 'Health and Community' building health posts in the Himal and training local staff to man them.

There is a new government now – a federal republic (I write this in 2009). Perhaps now, at last, things will begin to change. And there is good work on improving Education standards - Aiden Warlow, for example, whom I travelled with on a later visit to Nepal, has founded Kathmandu University High School up in Dhulikhel, an example of best practice which continues to set standards for the future.....

**

The back streets of Kathmandu are little microcosms of life, lived under the shadow of these tall buildings – corn cobs hang, and from tiny dark doorways, families spill out into courtyards where the real life of the community goes on in all its richness, far from tourists and the city life of Kathmandu. Sharma explains that many families have little fields beyond the city, one reason for the cloying, red diesel fumes from the home-made tractors which clog up the few roads into the city at dawn and dusk. Despite city living, this is still an agrarian economy.

We sit among decaying buildings, beautifully decorated with carvings, watching the street life in one of the little squares. Children play with a blown-up plastic bag as a football, and one tiny boy squats in the dirt, gravely filling his pockets with stones. As he stands up his trousers fall down! He grins with delight, empties his pockets, pulls his patched and ragged trousers up with a grand flourish, squats on his haunches once again, and begins the whole pantomime once more, absorbed in his private game. These children are the future of Nepal. They deserve the best we can give them.

We are wandering across Durbar Square. I am pouring out my concerns.

'Just begin with small things,' smiles Sharma one evening. 'Education. For you and for us. Begin to make changes. Your young people. Our young people. Your children. Our children. Make a difference. Make a connection!'

Torn between regret, sadness and relief, it's time for me to go home. Our eldest daughter is getting married. There are things to sort out. I miss the children and my husband. I miss my valley, with its clear, clean stream, and the beauty of my native mountains, even though I feel so at home here.

I have been writing poetry while I have been in the hills, inspired by this amazing land and its people. Now, before I leave, I find my way down into the basement of the hotel where there is a small Business Centre, so that I can type up my work. The manager helps me out. To my astonishment, as each poem is printed out, the Nepalese staff crowd round to read, asking if they may take copies away. I end up printing each poem several times. It turns into a bit of a party. When I come back next time, it is to find my poems are well-known in Kathmandu. One, in English and Nepali, appears on the front page of *The Kathmandu Post*. Later, Bed, who has set up a computer institute in Dhulikhel, asks if he can print them as a book (*Into the Lotus*).

The morning before I leave, I make my way down to the basement to thank the manager for his help. It is deserted and silent except for a small group of people, sitting in a circle in the middle of the room. Several are crying. One of them gets up to greet me.

'We are mourning our colleague,' he says quietly.

'Your colleague?'

'Yes, the manager here. He was a good man. Perhaps you met him. He died yesterday. Typhoid. It was very swift.'

Life and death, so close. He had seemed healthy three days before. So helpful and kind. We had laughed together and he had shown such interest in my poems.

'People write poetry about Nepal when they get home,' he said. 'But we never see it.'

***

Sharma tells me, 'There is something else for you to do before you leave.'

I haven't been back to Pashupatinath since that first trip, when I stared through the stone box cameras into infinity, while the smoke from the burning gnats spiralled up into the sky. Suddenly then, the Universe had, for a few seconds, seemed to make sense at last.

We take a 'tuc-tuc' down into the old city. That familiar, strangely sweet smell assails me. That and the crowds, the beggars, the chanting, the marigold wreaths on the water. Again, on the far side of the Bagmati river, there is silence, peace, made deeper by the distant sounds of ritual, devotion, grief and joy. I find myself profoundly affected as before. Yet I have been on a long journey before returning to this place.

Squatting in a little square at the corner of one of the old buildings, is a tiny brick-built cave with a domed roof.

'A very holy man, a Sadhu lives here. Many famous people come to visit him.'

I stand for a moment and look back at the scene beyond that dark, oily river which flows so close by, its banks swollen by recent rains. A body floats past on what looks like a bed of blackened straw. The corpse, a woman, is beautifully dressed in a red-gold sari. She floats serenely past, flowers heaped on her body, hardly marked at all by the pyre.

We duck inside the tiny entrance. It is flooded with light; candles lit all around walls which are decorated with newspaper cuttings and photographs from magazines. In the centre of the little chamber, a man with long white hair, dressed only in a dhoti, sits cross-legged. He ignores us as he chants to himself, fingering his beads. He has a Western face, pale skin, a hooked nose, and looks ageless – he could be anything from fifty to ninety. We sit cross-legged on the mat (always a struggle for me) and wait for him to notice us.

Sharma is entirely at home, his eyes closed, dark skin glowing in the candlelight against his usual immaculate white shirt. My legs are beginning to ache unbearably, when eventually the Sadhu opens his eyes, a startling blue. He looks fully at me, an unsettling experience.

Then Sharma speaks to him and seems to be asking for something. The Sadhu smiles and inclines his head. He speaks softly, gesturing around the walls with a graceful hand.

'The Sadhu says that many people come here to see him, many famous people. He himself has been to many countries. These are the photographs of his journeys, and of the many people he has met.'

I nod gravely, peering at the faded photographs stuck to the cave walls. Famous faces peer back – old politicians, pop stars, many I can't quite put a name to. The Sadhu is still talking.

'He lived on milk for thirty-five years, but he is very fit.'

The Sadhu winds his hair expertly up onto his head, smiles beatifically and winds his legs around his head. Then still smiling, he stands on his hands, in this tiny space. The candles hardly flutter. He comes back down in a lotus position, looking at me again with that piercing gaze.

'I have asked the Sadhu to give you a mantra, to take away with you to England,' says Sharma gravely. 'It is time for you to study Meditation. That is important.'

The Sadhu nods emphatically, then gestures to his primus stove squatting in the corner of the cave.

'But first you must take some tea with him.'

The Sadhu looks at me with his deep eyes and smiles. Squatting on his heels on the earth floor, he begins the ritual of making tea. He pours water out of a metal can into a saucepan, and the primus is lit, a blue flame. All around the candles dance in the dark cell. Beyond the open door, the brilliant sun beats down on old stone. I can hear the river rushing by.

Unbidden, the image of the corpse comes back to me, swirling and turning gracefully in the current. Where has the Sadhu got the water from? Surely not the sacred (but filthy) Bagmati River, with people floating past on their way to Mother Ganga and Paradise?

The water boils. Carefully the Sadhu pours it into three tiny steel cups on a decorated brass tray. I remember that other Sadhu in the hills – the grape he blessed and gave me, the long night of diarrhoea.

The metal cup is too hot to hold. As soon as my scalding fingers can manage it, I try to take a sip. But I am paralysed with fear. Is it the sight of the corpse floating in the river?

Sharma is looking at me.

'Let go and trust.' He doesn't say it but it's in the air. Yet I can't take even the smallest sip.

Sharma speaks to the old man. He answers gravely. Eventually, we get up. I can hardly stand, after sitting cross-legged for so long. I thank the old man for his hospitality, feeling an utter, craven fool. There is a saucer with a pile of rupees and I place some there. We walk out into the sunlight. Sharma isn't speaking to me. We walk up the steps through the shadows cast by ancient temple buildings. Monkeys screech at us. From beyond the river, the sounds of bells and chanting rise up into the sky. Halfway up the steps, the Sadhu, moving fast and very spritely, comes past with his billy-can. He puts his hands together in that ancient gesture of blessing.

'He is going to the clean water tap,' says Sharma, his voice heavy with reproach.

There is a pause while I labour up the stone steps in the sun.

'I'm sorry,' I say at last. 'I just couldn't. It was the woman in the river. I just kept thinking about the water.' It sounds so pathetic.

'The Sadhu says you are not yet ready to receive the mantra. When you return... perhaps.'

Perhaps? Perhaps an opportunity lost forever. So much of my life has been about being afraid.

Now, as I write, I still do not have that mantra, that gift from the Universe that was to be given so freely. Fear has always stopped me. But there is still time. And I have begun to study Meditation......

24

Time for me to go home and time to say goodbye to Sharma. He has done so much for me, taken me into his home, made me so welcome.

'I will come back. Next year, with the school. I promise I will come back.'

I am plunged into the boil of people beyond the airport gate. A chaotic scrum by the flight desk, my luggage well over the limit. Our daughter, Tessa is getting married at their homestead in Australia in a few months. In Thamil, I bought a beautifully decorated tin trunk to give her when she comes home for a blessing service. Heavy enough, but then I have added two copies of *Himalayan Flora*.

There is a nasty moment when an official tries to charge me US380 dollars for excess baggage, though it can't be anywhere as much as that. I am quite alone with no one to fight my corner. The weight counter seems to change from minute to minute. I don't have that many dollars on me. I don't have that much money…

'Aeroplane leaves in a few moments, madam. You must pay.'

At last (this was in the days before the widespread use of credit cards in Nepal) they let me through after taking all my dollars, pounds and rupees – about £200 in all. If I want to get on that plane, I have no choice.

I'm smarting with rage and humiliation by the time I get to the over-crowded, filthy, smoke-laden atmosphere of the departure lounge. All departures have been delayed. There is thick mist over the surrounding mountains and not even the STOL pilots who fly Royal Nepal will take the risk. So much for 'Your plane is leaving in a few minutes, madam!'

Hating Nepal, hating to feel helpless and vulnerable, hating the smoke, the filth, the corruption, I never want to come back, despite my idealistic promises.

Eventually I find a seat. I have fifty rupees and two English pounds with which to continue my journey. I blow all the rupees on a bottle of Coca-Cola.

I am tired already, though it's only mid-morning. I've been up since dawn packing that overstuffed suitcase. There are no seats left in the departure lounge and I perch on my luggage, disconsolate and disorientated. I will never be a good traveller – always over-packed, overstressed, worried about everything from germs to aeroplanes falling out of the sky.

I look around the room. There is a haze of smoke hanging like a pall over bent heads, exhausted travellers trying to snatch some sleep. Then I catch sight of a Buddhist nun on the far side, sitting bolt upright in her maroon robes, her shaved head is bent over her capacious handbag. As she looks up, I experience an unexpected thrill of recognition. I know this woman! I'm sure of it. But it's impossible. I don't know any Buddhist nuns. In fact I only know one nun of any kind. I continue to stare at her. She bends her head once again, searching her bag. I take a deep breath, and make my way through the body-strewn lounge. She looks up with that same abstracted air.

'Excuse me. I'm so sorry. You probably think this is foolish, but don't I know you from somewhere?'

She looks at me.

'Of course. You're Angela Locke!' Matter of fact, as though meeting me in the Kathmandu airport lounge is the most normal thing in the world.

'You came to interview the Abbot of Samye Ling – Akong Rinpoche – in Scotland. I was the nun who came in. Interrupted him to get a file, while he was talking to you.'

I remember the incident. The beautiful Tibetan monastery beside the banks of the River Esk, where I had gone to do some research for my book, *Dreams of the Blue Poppy*.

Ani Tsultrim Zangmo squeezes up on her single seat so that I can sit beside her, and we begin to talk, striking up an instant rapport. She explains now that she is on her way back from attending the enthronement of the 17th Gyalwang Karmapa, head of the lineage of Kagyu Samye Ling, at Tolung Tsurphu monastery in Tibet. She has been in retreat for six weeks in the mountains and is on her way home to Samye Ling monastery – less than an hour's drive from my own home.

I find myself pouring out my hopes and fears, and my modest plans for small-scale help in Nepal. She listened carefully while intermittently rifling through her handbag for her passport (which she is worried she has left at the airport desk). Eventually she locates it in the bottom of her capacious bag. We are able to relax together, chatting like old friends in the smoke-laden lounge. The mist lifts from the surrounding mountains, and we shuffle through to catch our flight.

We are at different points in the aircraft but once safely in the air, I see her sweet, stern face, topped with its dark shaven head, make its way between the seats towards me. She sits down, clutching her bag.

'Would you like to meet His Holiness The Dalai Lama?' she asks.

I am stunned.

'Of course. It has been my lifetime's ambition!'

'He is coming to Samye Ling over a weekend of 14th - 16th May. You could come as my guest. I will give you my cell. You would be very welcome.'

It's my birthday weekend. Ani (nowadays Gelongma) Tsultrim Zangmo is as good as her word. Thanks to her generosity, I am standing outside the temple when the Dalai Lama walks up the steps of the temple at Samye Ling, to the accompaniment of the deep vibrating burr of the radongs – those long Tibetan horns which resemble the alpenhorns of the Alps. Later, I am able to stand inside the temple for a special ceremony of blessing when HH The Dalai Lama, pauses briefly next to me, scattering rice around him. Later still, I am privileged to be in the great marquee to listen to His Holiness's speech, *Inner Peace is World Peace*. It is like a dream. I have to pinch myself. What a birthday present, to be here!

The whole place is ringed with a tight cordon of police security. No one is allowed in or out. Here on this day, too, are Chris Bonington, Doug Scott, and Chris's faithful climbing companion, Pertemba Sherpa (who lends me his umbrella), David Steel, the leader of the Liberal Party and many other political luminaries. It has snowed heavily overnight – three feet of snow in a day, very auspicious according to Buddhists. Almond blossom is on the trees. The roof of the marquee is buckling dangerously with the weight of snow, and streams of meltwater cascade down its sides. Yet His Holiness's laughter puts us all at our ease. Even the sea of mud which followed the heavy snowfall cannot dampen my spirits. I feel part of something extraordinary, at a special moment in time. And it's all thanks to that auspicious meeting in Kathmandu airport, and a diminutive nun with a great heart....

There will be other legacies of that miraculous weekend. The delight of having Gelungma Tsultrim Zangmo to stay with us, hearing that she had gone into the local pub in her robes while looking for our house (stirring up much local interest), of seeing her sandalled foot flat on the floor as she speeds back to Scotland, with me in tow. At Samye Ling there is an introduction to another amazing woman – Leah Wyler – Vice President of Rokpa, a Tibetan charity based at Samye Ling monastery, which work to help the street children of Nepal. Leah is almost six feet tall, a striking figure in her nun's robes and long, exotic ear-rings, with an arrestingly beautiful face. I am immediately drawn to her. With the then Abbot, Akong Rinpoche, she had founded 'Rokpa' – the Tibetan word for 'help' – after seeing hundreds of children living rough on the streets of Kathmandu, starting a children's home in Bhoudinath where more than fifty children have found safe haven. We too would become friends and some of our early work will be to help Rokpa's work with children in Kathmandu. There are indeed wheels within wheels in this small world.

25

A year later, I am back in Nepal with a group of Ullswater Community College sixth formers, sitting in the central hall of Sanjiwani Higher Secondary School. This is Bed's school, which I came to visit so long ago on my first trip to Dhulikhel. We are drowning in wreaths of marigolds (four or more each). All around me in the school hall are expedition members and those three teachers whose vision has made it all possible. The students, camped on a piece of flat ground just outside the village, will be taking part in activities at the school, and will help out with the building work in one of the classrooms.

Today is a day of speeches and welcome. Our doctor, Patrick Gray, who has agreed to be the doctor for the expedition, stands up to give a speech. His orange wreaths glow in the dim light. Everyone claps. Bed, my old friend, makes a speech of welcome. Everyone claps. A teacher from Ullswater Community College makes a speech. Everyone claps. It is the beginning of a happy accord.

In this place, on this day, real friendship will be forged and partnerships begun. Three of those expedition members, Karen Barbier, Sarah Barnard and Amy Holliman, will return to Nepal as our first volunteers, to work alongside street children with ROKPA in Kathmandu, distinguishing themselves with their compassion, love and deep connection with the country. All, like me, will have been changed profoundly by the experience of coming here.

But for now, I am a bit of an embarrassment, holed up in my bedroom in the hotel, having once again caught the Nepalese flu bug. I am confined to bed for a week with a chest infection, feeling left out and lonely, missing the singing and dancing and celebrations. Bed comes for breakfast meetings on the terrace of the little hotel in Dhulikhel, and Sharma comes to see me and cheer me up, in between delivering learned lectures on Nepalese culture to the expedition. Everyone tells me they are having a wonderful time. It's very galling not to be a part of it. I am due soon to go on a trek up towards Annapurna, while the students will be taking off in a different direction, towards Everest, but at the moment I have all the energy of a damp dishcloth.

Every time Bed comes to see me on the terrace, as I sit shivering in the early morning mountain cold, swathed in rugs and reeking of tiger balm, he urges me to go down to the little school in the middle of the town. They are waiting for me there, he says. I must not go away until I have been to see them. This was the school which benefited from the six hundred dollars I had brought out on the second trip from Ullswater Community College. Now that new classroom has been built and equipped.

Finally, I feel well enough on my last day in Dhulikhel to stagger down the hill, swathed in scarves.

I am totally unprepared for the welcome ceremony. The headmaster tells me that the teachers have been down to Kathmandu and have bought me a present. He hands me a picture of Durbar Square in beaten silver. On it is inscribed 'Present by Purna Sanjiwani Secondary School, Nepal to Angela Locke- England'. I am close to tears. I want to say 'You have no money for tables and chairs, yet you want to give me such a generous gift,' but I can't, because showing appreciation and giving in return, as with the little girl and the Juniper, is what the Nepalese people understand so well. Giving with the heart is what is important.

I have that picture still, in pride of place next to my Buddha and my Tibetan singing bowl, back in my valley in Cumbria. I look at it often, and remember those wonderful, generous people who had so little and gave me so much.

The day before I meet up with everyone on the Annapurna trek, the phone rings in my room in Kathmandu. Sharma is downstairs in the lobby and wants to see me. He seems agitated and upset. Last night Sita came home in tears after visiting a nearby school. Would I go and see it? He has a tuc-tuc waiting outside.

We travel across Kathmandu in the dusty heat. Still feeling washed out after the flu, I think longingly of my hotel room. I feel as though my head is stuffed with cotton wool. When we get near to the school, the road runs out. We pick our way down the back alleys. A dog lies in the dust, still alive, its face half-eaten with some awful disease. There is rubbish everywhere, a sour smell of deprivation, and an air of hopelessness normally absent even in the back streets of Kathmandu. It's usually such a happy place despite the poverty. Everywhere is shuttered, seeming unoccupied.

Sharma knocks on a wooden street door.

'Is this a school?' I ask incredulously.

'Yes, this is Shramik School. Shramik means 'labourer'. The school for the labourers' children. It's very poor. My wife came here yesterday. She came home crying.'

'And there are children inside?'

'Yes.'

A window opens on the first floor. A woman peers out, and she and Sharma have a shouted conversation. I stand in the filthy, dusty street, my scarf over my nose, head pounding. Another mangy, half-dead dog comes up to sniff my skirts, collapsing at my feet.

The door opens to reveal darkness beyond. I really don't want to be here, in this dim hopeless street, going through this dark doorway.

A woman, smart in a good sari, ushers us inside.

'This is the headmistress,' says Sharma. We *Namaste* each other gravely.

The wall in the stairwell is running with damp and mould. We clamber up, cautiously feeling our way, into a room almost as dark. I stand for a few moments adjusting my eyes. I still can't see anything. Yet the silence is broken by an underhum – the sound of children, the odd soft voice, an occasional giggle breaking a discipline of silence. Then an adult voice gives a command. There is a screech of chairs being scraped back, the sibilance of children standing up.

My eyes are adjusting. I see, to my amazement, children standing to attention, so many of them, everywhere in the dim blackness, hands raised together in the traditional greeting. Rows and rows of children crammed into the overcrowded space.

'*Namaste, Madam! Namaste, Sir!*'

Sharma is by my side.

'The school put jump leads onto the main cable in the street. They were fined!' He whispers. 'They could not pay their electricity. Now they still can't pay it. They are teaching in the dark.'

I can see the children more clearly now, in the dim light from the window. 'Please ask the children to sit down.'

'The school needs a new building,' Sharma says. 'They rent this land from the temple authorities. There is more land down the street. I will show you.'

I say goodbye to the children. In the darkness, I have begun to discern their smiling, eager faces. My heart turns over.

'*Namaste.* I will see you again! I will come back!'

The headmistress, other teachers, Sharma and I, walk out into the street in procession. One half-dead dog is still lying in the dust, while another waits patiently for me. The sunlight is blinding. I gulp down the thick air.

'What happened when they put the jump leads onto the cable? Wasn't it very dangerous?'

'Yes, very dangerous. And, I told you, the school was fined. Now they are even poorer.'

'But what can I do?'

'Tell your friends. Maybe they can help to build a new school.'

We walk on down the rough track, between wild mustard plants, yellow borders beside the dusky fields.

'This community is very, very poor. They pay for the children's school themselves. They would all help to build a new school with their own hands.'

It is quiet out here, on the city's outskirts, away from the stinking, rubbish-strewn street, the sick dogs (though one is still following me). Almost like being in the countryside. A good place for children to go to school.

The headmistress and the male teacher are talking to Sharma. He translates.

'They are asking the temple authorities for the land. Then they would build a new school. Can you help them?'

I smile weakly at their hopeful faces. My headache has got worse.

'Please tell them I will do my best. I will bring my friends. We will try to help. But I can't make any promises. I hope they understand.'

Next year, I am back in that dark classroom, with the Vice-Chairwoman of the fledgling charity we have begun. Ailsa Mackenzie is a dynamic individual whose energy has blown through the Trust like a benign hurricane. As we emerge from that dark place once again, the children's *Namaste's* ringing in our ears, I see the same emotions in her face as I felt on my first visit.

What can we do? We must do something!

First of all, we pay the electricity bill so that light can be restored into the classrooms. (we did this every year). We come out with paint and equipment to brighten the school. Beyond that, Ailsa personally pledges herself to fundraise for us for what will become 'The Shramik Project', our first big initiative.

***

However, trying to help, even with the best of intentions, is never easy and sometimes not appropriate. In the end, building a new school for Shramik defeats us. There are endless negotiations with the temple authorities, who own the land. More and more obstacles arise out of the blue. Things are always more complicated than they look. It is a sharp lesson for us all. But the money Ailsa and Juniper Trust raised for the 'Shramik Project' is ring-fenced to help the very poorest children of the 'untouchable' castes – though such caste distinction is officially outlawed in Nepal. These children often have problems finding places at conventional schools, which further emphasises their cultural isolation. Sharma's wife is instrumental in showing us where the greatest need is, and we build a new Ardesha school, rebuild Balodaya school for the children of itinerant carpet workers, and put running water and toilets into Lalit Bikash, Sita's own school, as well as making real improvements to Shramik School itself. The project still continues, as we fundraise for a new block at Ardesha, consider improvements to Balodaya, and continue to support the Helpless Children's school at Chobar, all this in the spirit of helping to bring the poorest children, those who have so little, out of the dark...

Epilogue

'Giving and Receiving'

I am awake suddenly in the night, back in my juniper-filled valley in Cumbria. I have been dreaming of Nepal, and in these dark night hours, I see something important, that the little girl on the mountainside at dawn had given me something even more precious than I ever imagined.

We have been searching for a name for our fledgling charity, which will express all we are trying to achieve. Aid can be about power, and is often disempowering for those it seeks to help. We have a vision of a charity which will receive as well as give: an equal exchange between friends. If I have learned anything from the Nepalese people – and I have learned so much – it is that we must give what gifts we have without arrogance, and learn to receive, to understand, with humility.

Wisdom, hospitality, generosity of spirit, and that deep spirituality which the Nepalese people have in such abundance, and which goes deep into the heart of Life – that, for me, is the lesson of the little girl on the mountainside at sunrise. In that moment I had nothing to give to her. She was the giver, and she gave to me, simply, sweetly, with a precious gift enshrining the sunrise. I simply had to receive, with gratitude. Now in the middle of the night, I see what is almost written up in front of me in dancing letters. The memory of the tiny girl who held my hand above Dhulikhel, and gave me a gift of Juniper, should always be remembered in the name for our charity, *Juniper Trust!* Juniper, that sacred herb, given by a child who had so little, to someone who had so much, a simple gesture of friendship. And Juniper grows here too, in Cumbria, in our own mountains. It will symbolise our part of the bargain.

In Cumbria too, Sir Chris Bonington agrees to be our Patron. And now, against all the odds, Juniper Trust gradually becomes a reality, forged with members of the Cumbrian community; doctors, climbers, teachers who share this common vision. The Trust will be about equality, about each of us giving what we can. Not about power, not about imposing ideas on other cultures, but about partnership and support, being there, for friendship for as long as friendship lasts.

***

At the end of the Juniper Trust meeting, I sit back and look out over the mountains beyond the little grey town of Keswick. The last light is just touching the tops of the higher fells in the distance, the sky still ringing with light. I think how lucky I am to live in this wonderful place, how lucky to have such fantastic people to work with on Juniper Trust, how far we have come. We are now working in so many places that I would like to visit. It would be good to see what we have done there, to help a little. But even if I never get there, I know that the young people, KE trek leaders, and representatives we have in so many countries, will keep the energy going for us all.

One day I may go back one last time to Nepal, perhaps to receive the mantra from the old sadhu beside the Bagmati River. Maybe this time I will not be so afraid. For if I have learned anything on this journey, it is that we are led gently where we are meant to go, despite our fears…

Angela Locke
Cumbria 2009

BIBLIOGRAPHY

On Nepal:

Into Thin Air, John Pilkington: George Allen & Unwin, 1985

Himalayan Solo, Elizabeth Forster: A Nelson, 1982

Window Onto Annapurna,: Joy Stephens: Victor Gollanez Ltd, 1988

The Wildest Dreams of Kew, Jeremy Bernstein: George Allen & Unwin Ltd, 1970

The Waiting Land, Dervla Murphy: Century Travellers, Arrow Books, 1990

A Guide to Trekking in Nepal (Fifth Edition), Stephen Bezruchka: The Mountaineers, Seattle, 1989

Nepal, Tony Wheeler & Richard Everist: Lonely Planet Publications, 1990

Himalaya, Adhvin Mehta/Maurice Herzog: Thomas & Hudson, 1985

The Mountain is Young, Han Suyin: Triad, Grafton Books, 1958

Annapurna, Maurice Herzog: Jonathan Cape, 1954

Tiger for Breakfast, Michel Peissel: Time Books International, New Dehli, 1966

A Winter in Nepal, John Morris: Rupert Hart-Davis, London, 1964

Education for Rural Development, Dr Kedar Nath Shreshta & Biswa Keshar Maskey: HMG Ministry of Education & Culture, Nepal

Shiksha (Annual Journal March 1989), HMG Ministry of Education & Culture, Nepal

The Art of Nepal, Lydia Aran: Sayayogi Prakashan, Kathmandu, Nepal 1978

Himalayan Flowers & Trees, Dorothy Mierow & Tirtha Bahadur Shrestha: Sahoyogi Press, Kathmandu

Nepal Namaste, Robert Reiffel: Kathmandu, 1978

Travels in Nepal, Charlie Pye-Smith: Aurum, 1988

On Tibetans & Tibetan Culture:

The Last Dalai Lama, Michael Harris Goodman: Shambhala,

Boston, 1987

Great Ocean: The Dalai Lama, Robert Hicks & Ngakpa Chogyman: Penguin, 1990

Inside the Treasure House, Catriona Bass: Victor Gollanez, 1990

Princess in the Land of Snows, Jamyang Sakya & Julie Emery: Shambhala, Boston & Shaftesbury, 1990

A Guide to Tibet, Elizabeth B. Booz: Collins, 1986

Tibet: Shangai People's Publishing House & Bracken Books, 1981

Tibetan Trek, Ronald Kaulback: Hodder & Stroughton, 1943

In Haste from Tibet, Rinchen Dakpa & B.A Rooke. The Travel Book Club, 1971

Secret Tibet, Fosco Maraini: Hutchinson, 1954

Seven Years in Tibet, Heinrich Harrer: Rupert Hart-Davis, 1953

Lhasa: The Holy City, Spencer Chapman: Chatto & Windus, 1940

Tibet is my Country, Thubten Norbu/Heinrich Harrer: Rupert Hart-Davis, 1960

Captured in Tibet, Robert Ford: Oxford, 1990

Tibetan Marches, Andre Migot: Hart-Davies, 1960

Tibet: The Lost Civilisation, Simon Normanton: Hamish Hamilton, 1988

My Journey to Lhasa, Alexandra David-Neel: Heinemann, 1927/Virago, 1988

Land of the Blue Poppy, F. Kingdon Ward, Cambridge University Press, 1913

General Background:

Mount Everest Reconnaissance Expedition (& other books) Eric Shipton: Diadem Books, London 1985

The Ascent of Everest, John Hunt: Hodder & Stoughton, 1938

Chris Bonington: The Climbers: BBC Books 1992

Tao Te Ching, Gia-Fu Feng & Jane English: Random House, New York, 1972

The Way of the White Clouds, Lama Anagarika Govinda: Hutchinson, 1966

Kingdoms of Experience, Andrew Greig: Hutchinson, 1986
The Turquoise Mountain, Brian Blessed: Bloomsbury, 1991

BOOKS

O is a symbol of the world, of oneness and unity. In different cultures it also means the "eye," symbolizing knowledge and insight. We aim to publish books that are accessible, constructive and that challenge accepted opinion, both that of academia and the "moral majority."

Our books are available in all good English language bookstores worldwide. If you don't see the book on the shelves ask the bookstore to order it for you, quoting the ISBN number and title. Alternatively you can order online (all major online retail sites carry our titles) or contact the distributor in the relevant country, listed on the copyright page.

See our website **www.o-books.net** for a full list of over 500 titles, growing by 100 a year.

And tune in to myspiritradio.com for our book review radio show, hosted by June-Elleni Laine, where you can listen to the authors discussing their books.

MySpiritRadio